Well done, good and faithful servant!

How to persevere with a faith that passes the test of time.

Steve Pollard

Well done, good and faithful servant!

Onwards and Upwards Publishers

3 Radfords Turf, Cranbrook, Exeter,
EX5 7DX, United Kingdom.
www.onwardsandupwards.org

First edition, published in the United Kingdom by Onwards and Upwards Publishers (2019).

ISBN: 978-1-78815-720-9
Typeface: Sabon LT
Illustrator: Steve Pollard
Graphic design: LM Graphic Design

Printed in the United Kingdom.

Endorsements

Steve Pollard's readiness to be vulnerable about himself as well as spelling out some of the great lessons of how to develop a genuinely Christian life, make this book an invaluable contribution. He brings a wealth of practical understanding of what goes on inside a person, drawn from years of in-depth counselling in which he and his wife have engaged. Moreover, this psychological insight is combined with careful biblical exposition to give a holistic view of how to grow spiritually. It is warmly to be commended.

The Reverend Canon David McInnes

In this profound, vulnerable and heartfelt book, Steve shows with eloquent clarity how we can achieve and enjoy a healthy inner life, one in which we become spiritually, emotionally and mentally free from some of the negative effects of past experience. To be able to identify some of the baggage that I have been carrying (in blissful ignorance) in my life and to be led through a simple method by which this is discarded (and replaced with something better!) has been an enormous blessing. I particularly love Steve's great practical advice for recognising and hearing God's voice in simple daily conversation. What a joy to relate to a God who loves giving short, direct answers to short, direct questions (I can feel His smile even as I write this!) And by combining common sense, holy truth and hard-learnt lessons from life, Steve's book offers a model of ministering to the whole person that is truly and enduringly effective. And the great news is, this model can work for anyone!

Revd David Frederick
Church Leader, Love the Street, Exeter

Helen and Steve have lived remarkable lives; both highs and lows. This incredible journey has inspired and motivated them to dig deep into how we're made and how we work as God's creation people who have been born into a fallen world. The insights and biblical wisdom Steve presents in this book provide a profound and practical roadmap to help us all understand ourselves better and learn how we can live flourishing lives.

Keith Johnson
Business Leader and Executive Coach

Well done, good and faithful servant!

There is such depth to this piece of writing, one that reminds us how real the spiritual battle can be. However, if we so desire, we can develop our relationship and intimacy with Christ. We can be confident that in our brokenness the Spirit can lead us to become warriors. I am encouraged by Steve Pollard, the practical approach and paradigm presented in this book, and that it helps us identify our inner being and walk toward freedom. I believe this work will enable more people to understand their purpose, experience renewal and empower them to multiply it in others.

Nigel Langford
Head of Church Relations for the Bible Society;
Co-founder and leader of Hub Church, Woodford;
Board Member; Westminster Theological Centre.

As a middle-aged white guy who earns a living through contractual law and whose father was in the Navy, I liked the autobiographical elements of the book. I appreciated the language and culture that was portrayed. The analogies are excellent, well explained and keep coming throughout the book. This ensures the reader is able to relate in many different ways.

I was familiar with the spiritual challenge of the book but found it useful to apply, once again, to my own life.

Altogether an enjoyable and edifying read, which should be read and read again.

Simon Clark
International Business Leader

Time spent with Steve Pollard is life-changing! At last, through this excellent book, a wider audience can benefit from the wisdom and understanding that God has given to him over the years.

I can personally vouch that the principles Steve unpacks here are truly transformational.

May the Lord use this treasure of a book to bring many people into freedom, intimacy with Jesus and fruitfulness for His Kingdom and glory.

"It is for freedom that Christ has set us free"! (Galatians 5:1)

David Edwards
Worship Pastor

This book is certainly not for the spiritually faint-hearted! Instead it is for those who are longing to go deeper in their understanding of who God has created them to be and to be better equipped to walk into the fullness of that. The depth of honesty and vulnerability with which Steve writes, alongside the clear biblical framework that he provides, creates a very safe, yet deeply challenging read for any believer. I found this book to be not only helpful for my own personal spiritual walk, but potentially powerfully transformational too...

Nicola Neal
CEO and Founder, Every Life International

What I most appreciate about Steve and Helen's approach is that they care for the whole person. We found it hugely beneficial and liberating to apply God's grace into our past, feelings, thoughts and spirit. In this sense, it was a new and much-needed paradigm for us.

It enables gospel-based, Spirit-led, personally-applied repentance and faith with a simple approach.

Stu Alred
Pastor, Grace Church, Exeter

If there is anyone who deserves the accolade from God, "Well done, good and faithful servant!", it's Steve Pollard. He is someone who walks the talk with exceptional faithfulness in life and ministry. He lives what he teaches on a daily basis through the highs and lows.

Over the last decade Bespoke ministry has brought release, transformation and hope to so many people. Some have reached the end of the line with nowhere else to turn. Others have been leaders who want to serve God more faithfully and with greater freedom and power.

Whether Steve and Helen are offering intense and profound ministry to the depths of people's trauma or simply helping people walk more closely with God, they never make it about themselves and their ministry. Their passion is for people to have the skills and insights to take responsibility for their own faith and walk. It is so fantastic to see their wisdom so clearly distilled and expressed in black and white. This book is a must for anyone who wants to live fully as a disciple of Christ. It offers profound insights for those who are broken and struggling to cope, alongside basic understanding that is essential for anyone who wants to live as God intended.

Revd James Grier
Vicar, Unlimited Church

Well done, good and faithful servant!

I met Steve and Helen when I was going through a very difficult season in my life. I found their gentle advice on how to bring my hurt, confusion and questions to Jesus and hear his answers to be incredibly life-giving. I commend this thoughtfully written and helpful book to you in the hope that it might do the same.

Andy Croft
Joint Senior Pastor, Soul Survivor, Watford

I couldn't put this book down; it is more than a useful text with teaching and advice for personal and client work, it is more than an autobiography. Steve's frank honesty provides the reader permission for their own vulnerability as well as a guide through to a hopeful outcome.

As an Integrative Counsellor who also works with women exiting modern-day slavery, I am so grateful for so much wisdom, theory, exercises and personal insights condensed into one easy-to-read volume.

Sue Clark (MBACP)
Integrative Counsellor and Salvation Army Modern-Day Slavery Support Programme Volunteer

Steve and Helen have been a huge help to us personally and to many in our church family. I commend this book to you as I commend their ministry to our church members! As you read it, I would encourage you to take your time over the questions, and allow the Holy Spirit to do his work!

Revd Edward and Lucy Hobbs
St Andrew's Church, Cullompton

A year after ending a long-term abusive relationship, I sat down with Steve as he guided me through the ideas and practices set out here. I want to say it changed how I looked at the situation, but really it changed the way I looked at myself; at my self-worth and self-identity, and my relationship with Jesus. Some of the things we discussed I still reflect on now and still benefit from. This is a valuable and worthwhile model, and one that I hope will continue to serve and release many people as they discover this book.

David Poulson
Youth Worker

All of us experience the tension between who we want to be and how we are actually living, whether because of major wounds or simply the toil of daily life. This book is for anyone who wants, with God's help, to step more fully into who they want to be. What Steve Pollard does so well is to make simple and clear some very big ideas about how the world works both in the spiritual and the natural; to draw together insights from different streams of counselling, inner healing and psychology into an holistic view of life; and then to bring from these practical tools for how to grow in God and walk into freedom. But *Well Done Good and Faithful Servant* is more than just another 'how to' book, it contains wisdom hard-won through Steve Pollard's own life and then honed through encouraging countless others to grow in God through the ministry of Bespoke. In other words, it's real stuff. You see, Steve Pollard is a trained spiritual director and life coach, a husband, father and grandfather; he has been a naval officer, solicitor, church leader and church planter; he has journeyed through long term mental illness, the loss of his first child, and multiple serious illnesses in his close family, to a place not only of healing but of helping others find freedom. And Steve Pollard is my dad. So much of what I know of following Jesus, living life well, being a husband and raising children, I have learnt from his invitation to share his journey (the good and the bad), to watch how he lives and how he learns, and to hear him speak into my life. In this book he extends that same invitation to you.

Sam Pollard
Associate Vicar, All Saints Woodford Wells;
Lead Minister, Barking Riverside Church Plant

Steve and Helen have been a huge help to us personally and to many in our church family. I commend this book to you as I commend their ministry to our church members! As you read it, I would encourage you to take your time over the questions, and allow the Holy Spirit to do his work!

Revd Edward and Lucy Hobbs
St Andrew's Church, Cullompton

About the Author

After serving as an officer in the Royal Navy, Steve Pollard went into Law and eventually developed a Medical Negligence and High Court practice as well as being Staff and Development Partner, building a sole practice into a successful two-office firm. He was also involved in church leadership as well as raising a family with his wife Helen.

Eventually, Steve decided to dissolve his firm to focus on the church work. However, during this period of transition, whilst setting up a medical negligence department for a sole practitioner, Steve had a breakdown due to workaholism. There then ensued a long period of recovery and redirection involving extensive counselling and rebuilding which has given him a unique experience of a shattered life and the arduous journey into building a new and better life.

During this journey Steve helped establish a counselling charity, becoming a counsellor and trainer of counsellors. He successfully completed Advanced Training as a Spiritual Director in the Ignatian tradition and ran retreats within the Manresa Link.

Steve and Helen had always believed their first ministry was to raise godly children and that it would be time for them to move into their particular ministry when they became independent. In the 1980s God had promised Steve that he would help the broken-hearted become brave-hearted. In 2006 when seeking clarity as to their ministry as a couple God reaffirmed that promise with a particular focus on youth, marriage and church, especially supporting leaders within their ministry and personal lives. Upon sharing this with their associate vicar, he invited them to join him and his wife to establish a multi-generational church in Exeter to support young people who "don't do church". After nine months of further training in prophetic ministry in London, Steve and Helen moved to Devon in 2008. The Lord blessed the enterprise and Unlimited Church became a Bishops' Mission Order in 2012. Steve and Helen withdrew from being part of the formal leadership in 2015 to make way for younger leaders but continue to play a supportive and mentoring role.

To earn their living, God led Steve and Helen to establish *Bespoke Growth in God* in 2010 under a Board to whom they are accountable. *Bespoke* style is a unique blend of prayer, professional expertise and personal experience.

Prayer includes extensive training in various forms of prayer ministry and spiritual direction, broad experience of pastoral care, and the gifting and leading of the Holy Spirit, with sensitivity to the breadth of Christianity from traditional to charismatic.

Professional expertise comes from a thorough professional training, and compliance with professional standards of Ethics and Conduct, including supervision and continuing professional development in accordance with their national accrediting bodies.

In terms of *personal experience*, Steve and Helen have each suffered and recovered from trauma, and from being on the receiving end of good and not-so-good instances of prayer ministry and counselling, both Christian and secular. This enables them to empathise with clients' struggles but also to be confident for their progress.

Steve and Helen are passionate about helping people deepen in the love of Father-God and to discover and walk into their unique God-given design and purpose. Where there are obstacles, they facilitate thier removal and ongoing walk into fullness of life.

Bespoke Growth in God serves individuals and churches from across the nation. One church leader describes *Bespoke* as a third level service, helping people who may be beyond the resources of the local church, with a respect for faith that is not possible within the NHS.

Jesus has blessed individuals and churches over the years through the ministry; *www.bespokepollards.com* contains some of their testimonies. Encouraged by their clients, Helen published some of her story in *Outgrowing the Shackles* in 2018 and this book is Steve's description of the paradigm Jesus has used to bless many.

To contact the author, please write to:
steve@bespokepollards.com

More information about the author
can be found on the book's web page:
www.onwardsandupwards.org/well-done-good-and-faithful-servant

Well done, good and faithful servant!

Contents

Well done, good and faithful servant!

Foreword by Paul Harcourt

There is a famous quote from A. W. Tozer, the early twentieth-century preacher and spiritual writer, that resonates with anyone who has pursued a relationship with God for more than a few years:

Christians don't tell lies – they just go to church and sing them.

For many of us, that quote occasions a wry smile. We know the tension to which it refers! We have been in worship, singing hallowed lines such as "All to Jesus, I surrender", whilst knowing (at least on reflection, if not in the actual moment) that there are many areas of our life where that remains manifestly not the case. I suppose that we could at least say that singing such a line is aspirational – in the moment of worship, captured by a fresh glimpse of God's grace, we would want to be able to say something like that.

There are also the times when what we are singing are someone else's experiences, inspired and recorded for us in scripture. For example, we have read and sung the faith expressed by David in the 23rd Psalm, but our faith sadly falls far short of David's.

The LORD is my Shepherd, I'll not want.

But I do still want for many things.

He makes me lie down in green pastures, he leads me besides quiet waters, he refreshes my soul.

But I am still anxious and know little of the peace and contentment that David is speaking about.

He guides me along the right paths for his name's sake.

But I most often feel that I am making my own way in the world, with little sense of his guidance and little awareness of how he is blessing me.

One of the great tragedies of our discipleship is the too frequent gap between our rhetoric and reality. Some of that is inevitable, for the reasons mentioned above, but too many of us are resigned to living well below the fullness of life that God offers us in Jesus. It doesn't honour

God to fail to lay hold of all he has for us and so show the world how good he is.

In one sense what we sing will always be beyond us until the Lord returns. In this life we have barely a taste of what he offers. However, we are meant to be growing into an ever-greater experience of this eternal life (the life of heaven, not just one that is long-lasting), which comes through "knowledge of God the Father and his Son Jesus" (John 17:3). To emphasise that this is the work of all three Persons of the Trinity, I believe that this is done in the power of the Spirit, whom Jesus said would "guide us into all truth" (John 16:13). The gap is due to our inability to grasp truth. All of us need inner healing from the lies that we believe about ourselves and about God. We need the Spirit's revelation.

Many have been immensely helped by Steve and Helen Pollard's fruitful ministry over the years. What Steve shares in this book is rooted in his own testimony, from spending time searching the scripture, and in cooperating with God's healing and restoring work. This is hard-won wisdom from someone who has refused to settle for less than God wants us to enjoy. He has gone deep and dug out great nuggets of truth to share with others, and I know that you will find things here to help you in your own adventure with Jesus.

Paul Harcourt
National Leader, New Wine England

Preface

Why this book?

To help you find answers to some vitally significant questions you may have.

- Am I intimate with Jesus, or just religious?
- Why does Christianity seem to work for others but not for me?
- Why do I keep falling short from being the parent/spouse/child or employee/employer that I want to be?
- As even many Christian leaders fall into sin, how can I avoid that in my own life?
- How can repeated sin patterns be overcome?
- How can I move from being a pew-filler to being a true disciple of Jesus?

Who is it for?

Anyone who wants to hear Jesus declare, "Well done, good and faithful servant! Come and share your Master's happiness,"[1] when they meet Him, as we all will.[2] This book provides understanding and tools to enable you to become aware of, and know how to overcome, possible weaknesses that could prevent you receiving that acclamation.

Where it fits

In *The Lord of the Rings* the wizard Saruman wanted to conquer Sauron and as part of his strategy he attacked the neighbouring Rohirrim who were ruled by King Théoden. They took refuge in the stronghold Helms Deep which was supposedly impregnable. Saruman knew it well because he used to be friendly with Théoden and he was aware of one weakness to Helms Deep. Under the very thick and strong outer wall there ran a culvert. He wanted to exploit that weakness so he designed

---

[1] Matthew 25:23.
[2] Hebrews 9:27.

the strategy of placing a bomb into the culvert. Doing so involved great loss of life in his own troops but it did blow a breach into the wall through which he was able to access Helms Deep.

Saruman was implementing a key principle of military warfare: know your enemy's weakness and exploit it. If the defenders had also known but defended that weakness in Helms Deep, the wall may not have been breached. We have an enemy who knows our weaknesses and exploits them. We are wise if we also become aware of our weaknesses and guard them.

This book seeks to give pointers towards areas of weakness that the enemy frequently exploits.

Word fulfilled

It is my practice, as part of my devotions, to pray through words the Lord has given Helen and me. Early May 2019, a few days before reading the sample print copy of this book, I came to a word He gave on 18th October 2010 following my 60th birthday in response to my thanking Him for the love, generosity and kindness I had received.

I had asked Jesus, "What do you say Lord?"

He replied, "I have shown you something of how We and others see and appreciate you this weekend. You are … I have shown you this so that you can move forward in confidence to be a channel of my love and healing in these coming days. Victory is Mine. I won it at the cross. Your role is to show others My love and victory can be theirs to enjoy, relish and live in. My children are often bound by the enemy's lies and are hopeless. You can bring them to Me who am their hope, release, life. I have fashioned you for this purpose. Together we will extend my Kingdom, drive back the enemy and bring my children into LIFE. Let's go, Stevie. Let's extend My Kingdom, release My children, let love and life flourish. Turn Baca into Springs of Life. That's why I died, why I chose and fashioned you and Helen. I'm the Rock. You rock together. So let's rock and roll. This week the best begins."

I was thrilled to read these words and to realise that October 2010 was when Bespoke Growth in God began. The love, victory, hope, release and life God promised has come to many, many as He has worked through Bespoke. Now He will continue that work through this book. I am excited and pray that you too will experience in even greater measure God's love, victory, hope, release and life.

Core Beliefs

These are core beliefs I hold, along with many Christians, which underpin this book. I state them at the outset so that you may know where this book is coming from, but you do not have to agree with these beliefs to find value in the book. You are, I'm sure, a person who relates to people. How well your relationships work will be influenced by how well you know how you and other people tick. So, even if you disagree with some or even all of my core beliefs, I'm sure you will find much value in reading on!

God

The one true God lives eternally in three persons – the Father, the Son and the Holy Spirit, who delight in a dance of love. In the course of that dance, Father, Son and Spirit conceived humanity.[3] From Psalm 139 and other passages our belief is that God did not conceive humanity *en bloc* but rather conceived each individual to dwell within a specific time and place, to have a unique design with a unique destiny. This we know as a person's Original Design. Some know it as their Kingdom Blueprint, others as their Spiritual DNA. The Trinity then created a universe and within that a world as the setting for mankind, a setting which He declared to be very good. There can be many debates as to whether He created through a word that instantaneously brought creation into being or whether He created through the process of evolution. We are not concerned here with how He created but rather why? Scripture indicates His purpose was that all people, made male and female in God's image, would each enjoy a love relationship with the Father, the Son and the Holy Spirit. They would care for creation, and together live and love in the dignity of The Family likeness.

---

[3] See Ephesians 1:4.

Satan

Christ taught the existence of a personality of evil. This could be because He accommodated His language to a gross superstition, knowing it to be such. That would be to deny His integrity. Perhaps it was because He shared the superstition not knowing it to be such. That would be to doubt His omniscience and reliability as a teacher from God. Or it could be that that teaching is not a superstition, but actual truth. This position completely vindicates Christ as to His integrity, omniscience and infallibility as the Teacher sent from God.

In *The Screwtape Letters* C. S. Lewis warned about two extremes of error to be avoided when considering demons. We can either disbelieve in their existence or we can believe they exist, but to an excessive and unhealthy degree.

Scripture shows that Satan is a fallen angel who leads many like him. He hates God but knows from experience that he is powerless against Him directly. He can pain God by seeking to destroy those God loves, man and creation.

His main tactic was to use temptation to achieve three goals.

- To beguile man and woman out of their relationship with God.
- By so doing they would surrender oversight of the world to Satan whom Jesus describes as the Prince of this world[4].
- All subsequent generations would be born as enemies of God. They would reinforce that by rebelling against God and the conscience He gives to each as a pointer to His truth. They would be under the dominion of darkness and blinded to spiritual realities, unable to receive gifts of the Spirit of God because those are spiritually discerned.

Satan achieved his goals.

Redemption

God's reaction to man's rebellion could have been one of anger, to wipe people out. It could have been one of power, to make them acquiesce to His will. Instead God chose a painstaking and time-consuming strategy of self-sacrificial love. We are living within that process.

---

[4] See, for example, John 12:31, 14:30, 16:11.

18

Two key aspects are already complete. One, God prepared a people into whom He could reveal Himself, Israel. The Old Testament of the Bible sets out this aspect in detail. Two, the second person of the Trinity took man's nature yet without sin, being conceived by the power of the Holy Ghost, in the womb of the virgin Mary. In this way the two whole, perfect and distinct natures, the Godhead and the manhood, were inseparably joined together in one person, Jesus. He – being, as the Westminster Confession declares, "very God, and very man" – is the only Mediator between God and man. The Gospels in the New Testament of the Bible describe how Jesus taught and demonstrated the truth of God's love and that God's Kingdom is "at hand"; how Jesus chose to die as man's substitute to pay the penalty due to each person's rebellion against God; how Jesus then rose from death showing that justice had been satisfied and through Jesus each person could be reconciled to God and reborn into His family. Jesus then ascended into heaven.

The culmination of God's strategy lies in the future: the personal and visible return of Jesus Christ in the full power and glory of Godhead to raise all people to judgement in which He will confirm and implement the choice each individual made during their lives. Those who chose to come to Him for salvation will join Him in the new heaven and new earth. Those who chose to reject Him will be released to live apart from Him who is the source of all love, goodness and peace. Jesus pictured that as a place of frustration, loneliness and pain. After all, the other inhabitants are Satan and his followers whose malice will not be held back by God's grace as it is at present. Those who find this objectionable need to recognise that our loving God must consider man's future to be gruesome if, in His omniscience, God could find no alternative solution other than His own searing self-sacrifice, and the suffering concomitant upon such a time-consuming strategy.

We live in the aspect of God's strategy that could be called 'the age of mercy'. God does not want even one person to perish so has endured Satan's malignity; people's mockery of and rebellion against God; their maltreatment of their fellows, each of whom God loves more deeply than a mother loves her child and whose pain pains Him; the exploitation and destruction of His beautiful creation. His forbearance is to give people time to turn to Him.

Jesus taught that the Kingdom of God is "at hand". So our age is also that of the 'now and not yet'. Those who turn to God are reborn into His Kingdom and are empowered to live in imitation of Jesus' character and ways 'now'. That Kingdom is 'not yet' fully established as we have seen it will be on Jesus' return. In the meantime, Jesus is interceding for people to heed His truth, to choose to live His way which is life in His fullness. More than this, He has sent the Holy Spirit to lead people into the truth. This 'leading into truth' involves the Spirit *revealing* that truth, *motivating* people to choose that truth, *empowering* them to live it and to conquer in the battle so they increasingly become like Jesus in character, speech and action until either He returns or they go to Him.

Battle

The prize is the vindication of God's strategy of self-sacrificial love as those who were under the dominion of darkness are drawn to choose to be born again of the Spirit and transferred into the Kingdom of Jesus.

The enemy's aim is to pain God by manipulating people to reject salvation in favour of the independence which Satan knows will result in eternal isolation from all that is good.

Whereas God chooses self-sacrifice, Satan is not loathe to use domination and 'darkness'. Jesus called him a liar and "father of lies"[5] which he uses to obscure the truth which gives light. He is deceptive. He accuses God to man (for example, to Adam and Eve he suggests God does not have their best interests at heart) and he also accuses man to God (for example, telling God that Job only served Him for what he could get out of God).

There are three areas of battle.

- One is direct conflict with the fallen angels. Gross aspects of this are seen, for example, in satanism and other occult practice, but more commonly seen is the spiritual conflict described in Ephesians 6 – about our battle not being against flesh and blood but against spiritual powers of darkness.
- Another is the world. We can see areas of the world where Satan uses the systems directly to oppress. There have been more martyrs in the twentieth century than in the previous nineteen centuries put together. Today there is an incredible number of Christians who are ostracised, actively persecuted and imprisoned for their faith, young Christian girls forced to convert and marry non-believers, people subject to honour

---

[5] John 8:44.

killings etc. Yet the enemy delights in oppressing any, not just Christians.[6]

In other parts of the world Satan deceives by alternatives, whether faiths that provide religion but deny Jesus; or 'isms': communism, secularism, rationalism, materialism, humanism and others. Jesus said you can tell a tree by its fruit. Pride, division, injustice, oppression of the many by the few, apathy, indifference, "charity begins at home" – some indicators of ungodly world systems, of battlefronts.

- The third area battle is the flesh i.e. our selves. Galatians 5 describes the flesh warring against the spirit, and the spirit warring against the flesh. Jesus highlighted this aspect of the battle because God's strategy is self-sacrificial love. It is essential for us daily to be victorious in the battle over our self because the last thing my self wants is to sacrifice itself for another – especially one as hostile, unappealing or simply 'other' as I was to Jesus before He opened my eyes to His truth and salvation. Without victory in this third battle, we will not engage effectively in the other two areas. This is why Jesus made the essence of following Him that, "…if anyone would come after me, he *must* deny himself and *take up* his cross."[7]

Many of us try to do this but we are hampered by the fact that we don't know how we tick, how we operate, how our self actually works. That lack of awareness is a major weakness; one that the enemy exploits just as Saruman exploited the culvert at Helm's Deep. The thrust of this book is to help us understand how we tick; to help us understand our self and so become

---

[6] Reported 19th June 2017 – "UNHCR's Global Trends report, the organization's major annual survey of the state of displacement, says that at the end of 2016 there were 65.6 million people forcibly displaced worldwide – some 300,000 more than a year earlier. 22.5 million refugees, the highest number ever seen. 40.3 million displaced inside their own countries. 2.8 million asylum seekers. On average one in every 113 people worldwide is someone who is displaced – a population bigger than that of the United Kingdom. One person becomes displaced every 3 seconds – less than the time it takes to read this sentence."
http://www.unhcr.org/uk/news/press/2017/6/5943ec594/war-violence-persecution-push-displacement-new-unprecedented-high.html

[7] Luke 9:23, emphasis added.

aware of our weaknesses. Then (unlike the Rohirrim whose wall was breached through their ignorance), led by the Spirit and with Jesus interceding, we will be enabled to take steps to guard against those weaknesses. We will prevent the enemy knocking us out of the battle. Even more, our God is so good that these weaknesses can actually be transformed into areas of effective service. We will no longer be under siege but moving forward into battle proving that the gates of hell will not prevail. Gates are structures of defence, not offensive weapons. If you long to prevail in the destiny God has uniquely for you, to gain a crown that you can throw at Jesus' feet for His glory, then read on.

Prologue

"I can't hold it!" I scream.

My hands are spread-eagled against the bonnet of a flatbed truck. I am pushing with all my might to try to stop it sliding down the drive. And pressing my feet as hard as possible into the drive – but they are still slipping! I look into the cab, into the eyes of my beautiful wife. She's holding tightly onto our baby boy while our girls aged three and one cling onto her, eyes wide with fright. I glance over my shoulder and see that we are nearer to the gaping hole in the drive. It's so deep and massive. Everything I own and all that is valuable to me is in this truck. I have got to stop it going down the hole!

I strain. I scrabble to hold my footing. I can't hold it! I look at my wife and children, see their despair as they realise I can't stop them going down the hole. My heels are over the edge. I leap to the side and as I pull myself away from the hole, I hear their screams.

I wake up. Helen is next to me, sleeping peacefully. It was only a dream. What a relief! Then, with as much impact as if I had heard a spoken voice, I realise this is a warning. If I don't do something, I will lose everything. But what can I do?

Well done, good and faithful servant!

I

Context

Well done, good and faithful servant!

CHAPTER ONE

Contradictory Christianity?

Christianity is not a religion following a moral code but is a relationship with a living, loving God. So why do many who would not call themselves Christian gain the strong impression that Christianity means a "thou shalt not" killjoy and deadening lifestyle? Why do so many other Christians hold so ardently to our disciplines and traditions as to drain all freedom and spontaneity from our devotional walk?

Jesus was a friend of tax collectors and sinners so why do the outsiders of our society feel that they could never come to church because they are not good enough and would not be welcome?

There is an amazing joy and intimacy in being born again into a relationship with the living God as His son or daughter so why are we so burdened and full of care, finding it hard to battle through from one week to another?

Jesus died to break the dividing wall of hostility between Jew and Gentile so that they might enjoy a unity akin to that within the Trinity, so how is it that we can be faithful attendees at church but feel that we don't really belong, no one really knows us?

Jesus was so freely Himself that He could fall asleep in the boat when others were straining at the oars; be so tired He rested at the well and sent His disciples into the village; be so grief-stricken that He wailed publicly with gut-wrenching cries over Lazarus. Yet we can be so inhibited that when in pain and asked, "How are you?" our reply can be, "Fine, thank you."

I am not pointing the finger at anyone here, as each of these examples is drawn from my own experience. We see similar contradictions in people in the Bible. Moses was the humblest of men but his angrily arrogant "Shall we produce water from this rock?" led to his not entering into the Promised Land. Elijah triumphantly withstood the King, his retinue and the four hundred priests of Baal, but ran for his life into depression at the threats of the Queen. Ananias and Saphira were truly born again but chose to deceive the apostles. Demas faithfully followed and suffered with Paul for years but then deserted him "in love with this present world".

Paul describes this contradiction in Romans 7 when he talks about not doing the good he wants to do but doing the evil that he does not want to do. It is part of the reality of being born again within a fallen world that is under the dominion of darkness and by which darkness we are each imbued and moulded. Even those of us who are aware of these principles find the struggle hard-going. Not surprisingly, many, like the church at Ephesus, lose their first love, and become lukewarm like the church in Laodicea. Perhaps a more painful experience is when those who've maintained the struggle for years and risen to influence in Christ's Kingdom are put out of the battle through some sin. When I hear of such, I feel, "There but for the grace of God go I," as I'm sure do many others.

Non-Christians can point to all of these and find reason to discount Christianity; we Christians can feel demoralised. I want to suggest that these are not indications of Contradictory Christianity but they are the expected implications of Campaigning Christianity. By campaigning I'm not referring to a fleeting political or social agenda. I refer to God's Campaign that He has been waging for centuries to wrest His good creation from the dominion of darkness and have His Son recognised and enthroned as the King of Kings; to enable each man, woman and child to share in His life every day and for eternity. The stakes are high. They are the eternal destiny of each individual. The battle lines are drawn. The enemy is ruthless, full of hate and lies, seeking to destroy. God has triumphed and will bring that triumph into everyday experience. The fly in the ointment is not that there are few who follow God, but rather that many of us who do, fail to recognise the battle, the enemy's agenda and the influential role played in our daily lives by that part of us which delights in darkness. Again, I'm describing myself. Jesus took me on a long and painful journey to bring me to the place where I not only recognised the battle, but enlisted; where I learnt ways that my self cooperated with the enemy and began proactively to wage battle against that self.

As Helen and I have shared these principles through our ministry, many have said that through them they have come closer to God every day, enjoying more of His abundant life. Our desire is that you too will live Campaigning Christianity.

CHAPTER TWO

My Journey

So let me introduce you to this journey. Born 1950 into a traditional Church of England family, I can remember as a little boy kneeling before my parents to say the Lord's Prayer before going to bed, but this stopped after a few years. My parents encouraged us to go to Sunday School, and I went to church parades whilst a Cub and then a Scout from nine to fourteen years of age. From twelve until my voice broke, I was in a church choir and went to Matins and Evensong each Sunday. Nevertheless, by the time I was fifteen I had abandoned Christianity. I could not accept the miraculous, particularly not a virgin birth or resurrection. I was widely read and formed my own belief system drawing on aspects of Eastern religions.

My parents encouraged me and my four siblings to advance ourselves, key values being success, hard work and not being weak and emotional. I was told I had to be a professional which, I was told, meant being an architect, a doctor, a dentist, an accountant or a lawyer. Teaching, which I would like to have pursued, was despised in my family, so was not an option. I had no aptitude for the first three and a week of trying to get my head round my brother's accountancy correspondence course showed me that that was a non-runner, so I decided to be a lawyer. I changed my grammar school to one where I could study A-level courses that would best help me access a law degree.

I was accepted by Sheffield University to study Law but in 1969 chose to defer my place for two years during which I would start four years of training to become a Royal Navy officer. The last two years would be at Naval College but I intended to replace those by applying for one of two university places available to trainee Supply Officers and, if successful, to take up my place at Sheffield University and become a lawyer in the Judge Advocates Branch of the RN. I was attracted by the security and variety of naval life but most of all by the sea, and was prepared to risk not becoming a lawyer.

Royal Naval training was a shattering experience. I enjoyed naval life and being at sea, but my value system rated academic ability far more highly than social aptitude. I discovered that being the second most successful cadet in my year counted as nothing for one as arrogant as I. As a midshipman spending a year at sea in a frigate, I was ostracised by the lower rank officers who could have been my natural companions. I don't blame them as I would have done the same in their place. After several lonely months in the Persian Gulf, on the voyage to Singapore I decided I would commit suicide on arrival. Fortunately, I went to the base doctor who prescribed medication. Supported by a couple of senior officers in the wardroom, I gained some emotional equilibrium.

I was selected to apply to go to Oxford University and flew from Singapore into an England in the grip of winter and the miners' strike. After interviews I was offered a place to study Philosophy, Politics and Economics but I turned it down, much to the chagrin of the retired admiral who organised the interviews. I preferred to take up my place at Sheffield to study Law.

I went to university with the goal of gaining a good degree to advance my career, and a wife. I had concluded from my suicidal period that the only thing that would make life worth living would be a good marriage. In those days, women did not go to sea in the RN, so university was my best opportunity to find a wife!

Within a few weeks I had met some people who spoke about having a personal relationship with God and whose genuine lives intrigued me. They invited me to a series of studies over three weeks to look at who Jesus was, what He said and what He did. I recognised that I had never looked at the evidence for Christianity as an adult and with an open mind, so decided I would join the course. After all, if what they said was true, it was the most important thing in life, and if it wasn't, I would have wasted only three weeks. Being me, I read widely and discovered that by the usual tests of historicity there was more evidence for the reliability of the New Testament than for many of the texts I had accepted as reliable when studying English, Latin and History. By the end of the course, I came to the conclusion that I would have to commit intellectual suicide to say that there was insufficient evidence to accept that the resurrection of Jesus Christ was a historical fact. As He had pointed to His resurrection as proof of His divinity, this meant I had to accept that He was God and therefore what He said about life was reliable.

I had been brought up to think that Christianity was a moral code but from these studies I realised that the moral code flowed from being born again by the Holy Spirit as a child of God. In my pride, to that time I had lived contrary to God's ways and in doing so had not only offended Him and hurt others but had broken His law. As a budding lawyer I knew that offence and hurt could be forgiven by the one offended, but that forgiveness did not remove the consequence flowing from having broken the law. That consequence is that God would honour my choice to be separate from Him. That meant eternal separation from God. As He is the source of all that is good, that meant an eternity without anything good. The Bible calls that hell, a place of lonely anguish. I realised that when Jesus cried out on the cross, "My God, my God, why have you forsaken me?" He had not been, as I had previously thought, asking for an explanation. He had cried out with the despair he experienced when, because He had taken upon Himself my wrong, and everyone else's, God withdrew. The resurrection shows that the full penalty has been paid and accepted by God, so that the way is open for reconciliation between God and anyone who believes that Jesus died for their sin.

I had read Revelation 3:20 where Jesus says, "Behold, I stand at the door and knock; if anyone hears my voice and opens the door, I will come in to him and eat with him, and he with me." In the culture of those times, eating a meal together was a sign of intimacy. This promise shows that Jesus waits for any individual to invite Him into their life to begin an intimate relationship. I had learnt that this is what being born again meant; that through the Holy Spirit I could be reborn into God's family.

Convinced that Jesus rose from the dead, and therefore was God, and therefore that His promise was open to me, I prayed in my room inviting Him into my life. I then sat back on my heels and realised nothing had happened. I tried again the next night, with the same lack of response from God, so later complained to the study leader that, "It doesn't work!" His reply was twofold. Firstly, God does not simply listen to our words but looks at our heart. If my intention was to use this as an insurance policy to secure a place in heaven, but in the meantime to live my own way, God would not respond as that would not be a true recognition of what this was all about. Secondly, he asked why I was sitting back on my heels and looking to see if anything had happened. By definition, God is truthful. If He says He will come in, He will, and the only appropriate response is to thank Him for doing so.

I went to my room and thought about my life. I realised I had made a pretty poor job of it so it made more sense to let God run it. I decided I would follow God as the leader of my life. I prayed again and admitted my pride and wrongfulness in His eyes and agreed that I deserved the penalty for that. I told Him that I believed Jesus had died in my place to bring me the possibility of reconciliation with God and that I intended to live the rest of my life for Him. I asked Him to come into my life, thanked Him for doing so and went to bed.

I prayed at 21:55 on 7th November 1971. When I woke the next morning, I was aware of an amazing feeling of security as if I had been climbing a sheer cliff face without ropes but had suddenly been lifted onto the safety of the top of the cliff. That feeling lasted for about three days before it gradually subsided. I am very thankful that I became a Christian within the context of people who not only helped you become a Christian but then showed you how practically to develop your relationship with Jesus and continue to live for Him.

This was the start of LIFE! Immediately there was such a transformation. Most of my childhood we had black-and-white television and I vividly remember the difference in quality when I saw my first football game on colour television. Being reborn by the Holy Spirit as a child of God was a similar transformation in quality. My daily activities from 8th November onwards were the same as up to the 7th but the quality was vibrantly enhanced.

So what happened, that some thirteen years later God had to give me such a drastic warning to catch my attention?

The lovely people who introduced me to Jesus held that the Bible is authoritative and inspired by God, to help us develop and deepen in our relationship with Him. I studied it, memorised it and fashioned my life upon it. Within a couple of years, I had committed my life to follow Jesus as not only my Saviour but also my Lord. He was very good to me.

In my second year at university He clearly led me to resign from the Royal Navy. Although this was a difficult decision which led to my parents cutting me off for some time, Jesus sustained me very intimately. For example, when I returned to my room after that painful telephone call with my parents, the psalm in my daily reading was 27:10 which reads, "Even if my father and mother abandon me the Lord will take me up."[8]

---

[8] RSV.

He also acted very powerfully in answering prayer. For example, in the Royal Navy I smoked sixty-five king-sized a day and was aware that my lungs were affected but I had been unable to stop smoking. Within three months Jesus had taken the desire for nicotine away completely.

When I left the Royal Navy, my father refused to complete the forms that would enable me to get a grant so although my fees were paid, I only had £50 per annum to live on to the end of my degree. God provided for me in varied ways, some quite marvellous 'God-incidences'.

I was still very keen to find a wife. As I searched, I learnt that the scriptural injunction not to be yoked with unbelievers[9] did not simply mean only to marry a Christian girl, but also only one with a similar heart and calling. Those lessons meant some relationships had to be broken. This was so painful that when God clearly showed me that He would provide my wife, and until He brought her to me I was to treat all girls as sisters, I agreed. After a few years I did wonder, but God told me He had it in hand. In 1978 He 'brought' Helen to me and we were married six months later – finally the groom, after seven times as best man!

In my career as a solicitor I chose not to find jobs in the Lake District or Peak District where I could pursue my hobbies of walking and potholing but instead only applied in areas where I could continue to be discipled and best serve Jesus. He honoured those decisions and by the time of the Prologue dream, I was the litigation and development partner in a firm of Birmingham solicitors. He had also given me positions of leadership within the Christian group and subsequently within Anglican churches.

To onlookers, and to me, mine was a success story. You will recall our key family values included success and hard work. My parents, seeing I had honoured those, had been reconciled to me, even buying my Lay Reader's stole when I was ordained. (As an insight into God's tenderness, there was only one scripture in that service: Psalm 27! I realised that when I had been weeping over that psalm, the Trinity were aware that the day would come when my parents would be supporting me in my faith. God knows the end from the beginning, so we can trust Him when the path seems strange.)

Yet this 'success' was only in career, status, income and ministry. These seemed so important, but I now recognise they are not the most

---

[9] See 2 Corinthians 6:14.

significant aspects of life. I worked hard to pursue success and I had been devastated when, sometime before this dream, God showed me that I had made commitment an idol. What I thought was living for His glory was in fact living to mine. There was a high price to pay for this level of hard work. That price was being paid by me but also by my wife and children. Although I professed that they were my first priority after Jesus, the way I lived showed that they came much lower down my list of priorities.

My arrogance that had led to my being ostracised by the wardroom had lessened as I grew closer to Jesus, but I am humbled and grateful when I look at my first decade as a Christian; humbled in that I can see repeated instances of relationship difficulties when I perceived someone had not treated me properly; grateful for those who continued to love and support this frequently very prickly pear. Most of all I am amazed by Helen's faithful and constant loving support.

I don't know if you have ever read *The Voyage of the Dawn Trader* by C. S. Lewis. One of the characters is an obnoxious lad, Eustace, who, among other things, is very greedy and finds himself transformed into a dragon. Aslan shows him that he needs to bathe in water and scratch the dragon skin off if he wishes to become a boy again. Eustace tries but is unable to scratch sufficiently deeply. Aslan offers to scratch the skin off for him. Eustace agrees and although the process is extremely painful, it is well worth it because he not only becomes a boy again but is actually an admirable young lad.

In many ways I was a Eustace. I was aware that I was not the person I wanted to be, but I did not realise that I was a dragon and needed my skin shedding. The Prologue dream was the revelation that shocked me into realising that my position was far more serious than I had realised.

I woke with a deep desire for the dream not to become my reality. I would love to say that this desire was the start of a determined and intentional growth into intimacy with Jesus but that would not be true. My desire was genuine and deep, but my life was busy and highly committed to established patterns. Although I did not recognise these obstacles at that time, Jesus responded to my desire and began to lead me into new ways. I tended only to recognise His design through hindsight. Not really the proactive paragon but more of a, "Duh, so that's what you've been doing."

I have described how Jesus revealed Himself to me and brought me into a part of His family that held a high view of the Bible. They really believed that the Bible was not to be interpreted by one's own understanding (such interpretations being, in their view, the failing of the liberal wing of the church). Yet they were of a cessasionist persuasion, which means that they believed that when the canon of the New Testament had been completed, God had withdrawn His spiritual gifts of prophecy, miracles, healing, speaking in and interpreting of tongues, and an emotional intimacy with Jesus through the Holy Spirit. I had adopted that cessasionist belief. One of the first new ways Jesus brought into my life was helping me to realise that in holding that belief, I too was placing my interpretation of scripture over what it clearly says. When I repented of that, God brought me into a fuller relationship with the Holy Spirit and taught me how to grow in His gifts.

Another new dimension which He opened to me was that of the reality of spiritual beings. On different occasions in the previous years He had prodded me in that direction, but I preferred to think in terms of the general force or power of evil and the negative consequences of selfish human behaviour. I certainly did not accept that a born-again Christian could be significantly influenced by a supposedly evil creature. That was until God led me and my family to Spring Harvest. I went to a seminar on spiritual warfare and was fairly sceptical throughout. At the end, the speaker invited people who had any involvement with Freemasonry to stand for release through prayer. I didn't have any directly, but Helen's father was deeply involved and the speaker said "any involvement" included that of a spouse's family. I stood. He prayed. I found myself on my back on the floor having been thrown over the row of seats in front of me. When I stood after the prayer, I was aware of the difference but this became more concrete when we got into the car to drive home. At Spring Harvest you park your car and only return to it at the end of the week. On the way in we had been listening to a worship tape. I had not been able to distinguish the lyrics. When I switched on the engine and it started to play, I could hear the lyrics very clearly. My hearing had been hindered by the spiritual oppression! Needless to say, this changed my theology and over the following months we saw much increased freedom within our family as Jesus led us to take the spiritual realm and its effect upon us and our children more seriously.

Jesus led us to join the Teamwork stream of house churches and through various circumstances the time came when I was advised to seek counselling. I was very reluctant to do so as I was afraid that if I began to 'look inside' I could well end up in an asylum. Sitting on the settee in our lounge, I remembered that after being a Christian for a year I had promised God that I would go anywhere for Him. I had meant geographically, but if He now wanted me to go on this interior journey, and even if it meant I lost my mind, I decided I would keep that promise.

Another factor was that a couple of years after I became a Christian God had promised me that I would serve Him by helping those who were broken-hearted become brave-hearted warriors. For several years I had been aware that I had built such protections around my heart that I was in fact hard-hearted, and I had been praying that God would fulfil for me His promise in Ezekiel 36:26: "I will take out of your flesh the heart of stone and give you a heart of flesh." On that settee I realised the way of receiving a heart of flesh, and being able to help the broken-hearted become brave-hearted, was for me to experience what that journey involved. So I agreed to be counselled.

God was gracious and I was counselled by John Bedford, a Birmingham minister who had been trained by Frank Lake, one of the pioneers of the inner healing ministry. With John's help I began to grow in emotional literacy and also to be less driven, but I still had a breakdown in September 1990. I was so ill that I 'lost' three months, but in January 1991 God led me onto a course through which He revealed to me a trauma I had experienced aged about two which had shattered my heart. This had led me to build protective layers, as we all do. Others who suffer a nervous breakdown recover more swiftly but with hindsight I can see God wanted me to go to my deepest roots so that I would not only learn about breakdown and healing but also have lived that journey. There then followed a fourteen-year journey of experiences with Christian counsellors and prayer ministers, and with the NHS mental health services, that was a mixture of good and bad from both. This book contains some of the lessons Jesus taught me through that journey.

For more than forty-five years I have lived with Jesus: through resignation from the Navy; prosperity as a lawyer; a wonderful marriage; three marvellous children and six grandchildren; the death of our firstborn; my wife suffering cancer six times (and being healed!); my becoming a workaholic with resulting breakdown from which I took fourteen years to recover, through the majority of which we lived on benefit and health insurance. Through it all Jesus has led, sustained, been very faithful and increasingly close. He has been true to His promise in John 10:10: "I came that they may have life, and have it abundantly." This is LIFE which continues for eternity. Once you come to realise how loving and 'for you' God is, that He is always with you and longs for you to co-operate with Him, you can walk into the exhilarating life He intended for you. I am confident that wherever you are on your journey through life, Jesus is able and willing to draw you into deeper intimacy and greater fruitfulness. Whether your heart is broken, or so hard that it doesn't trouble you, my prayer is that the Spirit will lead you to become His brave-hearted warrior. If you already are such a warrior, may He use this book to enhance your prowess.

Well done, good and faithful servant!

II

Paradigm

Well done, good and faithful servant!

CHAPTER THREE

Intel

"SYRIA ATTACKS ISRAEL!"

No, this is not a headline from the Yom Kippur war, 1973; nor about Syria's response to Egypt's request for help in the 1967 war; not even a reference to the 1948 Arab-Israeli war.

It could have been written several times during the period 885 BC - 865 BC as Ben-hadad, king of Syria, repeatedly attacked Jehoram, king of Israel. 2 Kings 6:8-12 describes how Jehoram "saved himself ... more than once or twice" from ambushes Ben-hadad had laid. Ben-hadad thought he had a traitor in his camp but his officers told him that, "Elisha, the prophet who is in Israel, tells the king of Israel the very words you speak in your bedroom."

Where one of two opposing parties is ignorant of strategic information, he is likely to be defeated. God did not want Jehoram to be defeated so, through the prophet Elisha, gave Jehoram vital intel about the location of the ambushes, enabling Jehoram to avoid them.

Many of us suffer defeats as we journey through life because we do not have vital intel that would enable us to avoid ambush or to battle victoriously against the enemy's strategems. There is a whole aspect of the battlefield which is a blind-spot for many; namely, how we as people function. The paradigm that follows is a layman's description of intel about how people function. We have seen many instances where God has used this intel to enable people to 'save themselves more than once or twice' and to enjoy more fruitful life journeys.

Paradigm

There are over 460 models of counselling, numerous ways of coaching, various models of prayer ministry. Much valuable work can be achieved by being guided by a practitioner in any of those. This can result in a person repeatedly consulting the practitioner when difficulties arise.

Well done, good and faithful servant!

Our ministry is called *Bespoke* Growth in God because we do not follow any particular model. Instead, one of our values is to hear where the client believes Jesus is leading them and then to draw on our experience and expertise to help the client follow Jesus. We are Bespoke *Growth in God* because we do not want to become the practitioner expert to whom a client repeatedly returns. Rather, another value is to give our client the understanding and tools that will enable them to grow in God and in their own ability to handle with Him the various difficulties they encounter.

This understanding, our paradigm, is about who people are and how they function. We do not claim particular originality. The paradigm is scriptural and therefore aspects may well be familiar to those who have experience of any of the current prayer models. It also reflects aspects of psychology, neurology and child development, so again, aspects may well be familiar to those with experience in any of those fields. What we do recognise is that most people reach adulthood without clarity about who they are or an understanding of how people function. Our hope is that this intel will be useful to those.

There are seven aspects to our paradigm.

1. We believe every individual is created to be a spiritual being (chapter 4).
2. We believe everyday communication with God is the birthright of every Christian (chapter 5).
3. We recommend a holistic understanding of how God has designed us to function (chapter 6).
4. We recognise a cycle which God has built into every individual by which they learn – this is known as the Belief-Expectation Cycle (chapter 7).
5. We recognise how people function (chapters 8-12).
6. We recognise the dichotomy within each of us (chapters 13 and 14).
7. We recommend the tool of repentance which will be familiar to most Christians but certain significant aspects of which are honoured more in the breach than in the observance (chapter 15).

The following chapters will explain the various strands of this intel and show how they can be used in everyday life. Our prayerful intention is that ordinary people will be able to 'save themselves more than once or twice' in areas where previously they have been ambushed and defeated.

CHAPTER FOUR

Intended to be Spiritual Beings

[At the burning bush Moses asked God], "Suppose ... they ask me, 'What is his name?' Then what shall I tell them?" God said to Moses, "I AM WHO I AM ... This is my name for ever, the name by which I am to be remembered from generation to generation."[10]

God is self-existent

He is life and the source of all life. In His High Priestly prayer, Jesus prayed, "Now this is eternal life: that they may know you, the only true God, and Jesus Christ, whom you have sent."[11] We use 'eternal' as an adjective of quantity meaning to continue forever but here Jesus is also using it as an adjective of quality. He describes eternal life as an intimate relationship with God.

God is Spirit

In conversation with a Samaritan woman, Jesus said, "God is spirit, and his worshippers must worship in spirit and truth."[12] Here Jesus is saying that only worship which is in and through God's Spirit and based on God's truth is acceptable to God.

God made people to be spirit

God created people "in the image of God"[13] then breathed into man: "...the LORD God formed the man from the dust of the ground and breathed into his nostrils the breath of life, and the man became a living

---

[10] Exodus 3:13-15.
[11] John 17:3.
[12] John 4:24.
[13] Genesis 1:26-27.

being."[14] The words 'breath' and 'spirit' are translations of the Hebrew word *neshamah* and the Greek word *pneuma*. The words mean "strong wind, blast, or inspiration". *Neshamah,* God's Spirit, imparts spirit into the created body and is the source of life that vitalizes humanity.[15] Upon death the "spirit returns back to God who gave it"[16].

At this point there is intimacy in the spirit between God who is Spirit and Adam and Eve who are also spirit. God, Adam and Eve enjoy the quality of life together that Jesus described in His High Priestly prayer.

Man rebelled

When Adam and Eve exercised their creativity and free will and chose to believe the enemy's appeal to their pride and appetites and insinuations against God rather than to love God by trusting and obeying Him, their ability to fellowship with God was broken. They no longer had, or were able to have, a Spirit-spirit relationship. They did not die physically that day but did *die spiritually.*

Ever since, the human spirit has borne the effects of the fall. Before salvation, a person is characterized as spiritually "dead"[17].

Rebirth is vital to restored relationship with God

Nicodemus, a member of the Jewish ruling council, came to Jesus at night and declared that he recognised Jesus to be "a teacher who has come from God. For no one could perform the miraculous signs you are doing if God were not with him."[18] Taking Nicodemus at his word that he recognised Jesus' teaching as being from God, Jesus gave him a 101 in salvation. He said, "No one can see the kingdom of God unless he is born again. ... No one can enter the kingdom of God unless he is born of water and the Spirit. Flesh gives birth to flesh, but the Spirit gives birth to spirit. ... Just as Moses lifted up the snake in the desert, so the Son of Man must be lifted up, that everyone who believes in him may have eternal life."[19]

---

[14] Genesis 2:7.
[15] See Job 33:4.
[16] Ecclesiastes 12:7.
[17] Ephesians 2:1-5; Colossians 2:13.
[18] John 3:2.
[19] John 3:3,5,6,14.

The 101 is:

- You must be born again of the Spirit.
- This rebirth is solely the work of the Spirit.
- It is only possible because the Son of Man (Jesus) will be "lifted up" i.e. crucified, as a substitute for any individual who looks to Him, which is the relevance of "the snake in the desert". Nicodemus will have been very familiar with that part of his people's history where they maligned His motive in rescuing them from the Egyptians and detested His provision. God punished them by sending venomous snakes whose bite brought death. When "the people came to Moses and said, 'We sinned when we spoke against the LORD and against you,' ... [t]he LORD said to Moses, 'Make a snake and put it up on a pole; anyone who is bitten can look at it and live.'"[20]
- This rebirth renews the Spirit-spirit relationship between God and man. Eternal life begins.

Two peoples

Everyone is born as one of those who are characterised as "spiritually dead". This does not mean that they are not spiritual. Every human being has a spirit, the incorporeal part of man that gives consciousness of self and the unique ability to comprehend and understand.[21] It includes our intellect, emotions, fears, passions, and creativity, free will.

When anyone believes in the "lifted up" Jesus and accepts him as their saviour, the Holy Spirit of God joins with their human spirit in ways we cannot comprehend. The apostle John said, "...we know that we live in him and he in us because he has given us of his Spirit."[22] When we allow the Spirit of God to lead our lives, the "Spirit Himself testifies with our spirit that we are God's children."[23]

The two peoples are: the spiritually dead who have not yet "looked to" Jesus; and the spiritually reborn who, as children of God, are no

---

[20] Numbers 21:7-8.
[21] See Job 32:8,18.
[22] 1 John 4:13.
[23] Romans 8:16.

longer led by their own spirit but by God's Spirit, who revitalizes their spirits and renews them day by day.[24]

The most fundamental issue for each of us is: who leads today, me or the Holy Spirit?

If we are not led by the Spirit, He has to send us intel indirectly. Is that perhaps why sometimes we are less victorious than we would like?

Exercise

Some people find exercises helpful so, where appropriate, I include questions. Please feel free to answer them or ignore them as you prefer.

1) Do you agree with the subheadings in this chapters, the statements in bold?

   If you do, spend some time thanking God that He has revealed His truth to you.

   If you do not, would you like to explore them? If so, there will probably be a church near you running an Alpha course, which is a series of interactive sessions that freely explore the basics of the Christian faith. No pressure. No follow up. No charge.[25]

   If you prefer reading, then any of these could help.

   a) The *Gospel of John* or the *Gospel of Mark* (in modern translation, not ancient English). In our desire to convince people that Christianity is true, we sometimes miss the power of personally encountering God's word.

   b) *Mere Christianity,* by C. S. Lewis.

   c) *More Than A Carpenter,* by Josh McDowell.

   d) *The Reason for God,* by Timothy Keller.

   e) *Simply Christian,* by N. T. Wright.

   f) *The Case for Christ,* by Lee Strobel.

   g) *The Reason Why Faith Makes Sense,* by Mark Mittelberg.

2) To which of the two peoples do you belong? Why is that a good place to be?

3) Whom did you follow throughout today? Yourself or the Holy Spirit? What would you change tomorrow?

---

[24] See 2 Corinthians 4:16.
[25] *https://alpha.org*

CHAPTER FIVE

Communication with God – Our Birthright

How does the Holy Spirit lead us?

It has been a feature of my Christian journey that, although I was reborn in an environment where the Bible was taken literally and as authoritative, I have repeatedly interpreted scripture in such a way as to deny myself the benefit of what it clearly states. I've mentioned already that for many years I believed the completion of the canon of scripture meant that the Holy Spirit no longer operated through spiritual gifts. This interpretation meant I restricted myself from the gifts and level of intimacy He wanted for me.

It was even later in our walk together that He showed me that although in Hebrews 6:1-2 Paul talks of the laying on of hands as a foundational teaching, I had reinterpreted that as being fulfilled in the 'extension of the right hand of fellowship' by the minister when a person became a member of the church. That also had restricted my expectation of how to experience Christ.

Similarly, although in John 10:4 Jesus clearly states that His sheep know His voice, I was in my fifties when I discovered I had limited His meaning. Until then I had only expected to hear His voice by experiencing His inner conviction of sin; by His bringing the Bible alive so that I saw His ways and heard His voice as I read it and heard it expounded; by His making scripture specially alive and pertinent so that through it I received His support and encouragement, admonition and correction, inspiration and specific promises for my adventure with Him; by His guiding me in how to pray and in His answering those prayers. What I did not do was to expect John 10:4 to mean 'what it says on the tin', that as one of His sheep it is my birthright to recognise and hear His voice. In other words, I can ask Him a specific question and hear His specific answer. Recognising that He did mean that revolutionised my relationship with Jesus and added zest to everyday life.

Another one of my reinterpretations was how I read Luke 9:23 where Jesus said, "…take up his cross daily and follow Me." I interpreted this as if Jesus said, "…take up his cross daily, read the scriptures and from my life draw principles of how I lived, and follow them." A direct result of this reinterpretation was that I lived by principle and rule rather than by relationship. Isn't that an accurate description of a Pharisee? When I started to believe John 10:4 meant that I could hear His voice, I was able to understand Luke 9:23 to mean, 'take up your cross daily and follow *Me'*. Which of us walks with a friend without conversation? Walking and talking with His friends was a substantial part of Jesus' lifestyle. We similarly can walk and talk with the Holy Spirit through our daily journey. One of the most frequent and delightful experiences for our clients is to discover that they can ask the Holy Spirit specific questions and receive His specific answers.

How do we hear His specific answers? Occasionally a person will hear an audible voice but this is quite rare. Most often the person will see a picture, have a thought, experience a feeling. Usually these will be a 'still, small voice' and therefore easily overlooked, and the enemy will be keen to encourage the client to rationalise them away as he most certainly does not want anyone to begin to live in the truth of John 10:4.

But someone might say that surely such impressions could be something other than the voice of the Holy Spirit? Yes, they could. We have many 'voices' speaking to us all the time: our environment; our appetites and body (i.e. our flesh); our fears, feelings, cognitions (i.e. our soul); the enemy; as well as the Holy Spirit.

To be able to 'tune in' more accurately to the Spirit's voice we need to tune out those other voices. Distractions from our environment? Turn off the muzak, move to where you are less distracted. Our flesh and soul? Ask the Holy Spirit if there is any specific sin with which we need to deal. One of His roles is to convict of sin[26] so He will tell us if sin is muddying our relationship with Him. We then clear that through repentance and confession.

An aside: you can distinguish between conviction from the Holy Spirit and condemnation from the enemy in that the Holy Spirit will always be specific and there will be a clear way forward whereas the enemy will speak in generalisations that leave you feeling bad. If you hear, "It was unkind of you to speak to Emily like that," usually soon after the

---

[26] John 16:8.

conversation, that is probably the Holy Spirit. If you hear, "Call yourself a Christian when you behave like that?" possibly sometime later when you're no longer clear what 'that' is, it is probably the enemy.

When free from distractions and sin, we would pray along the lines, "We bind our flesh, anything soulish within us, and in the name and authority of Jesus Christ bind any spirit which would interfere with our hearing God clearly." This 'clears the interference' so that we can more safely expect what we hear to be revelation. Even so, we recognise that we are on a journey into intimacy with Christ and what we hear will be a mixture of the Holy Spirit and ourselves. It is therefore important to weigh anything we hear against scripture and, especially if the subject matter is significant, to run what we hear past godly people whom we trust.

As you will see later, there are occasions when we do want to listen to each 'voice', note what it is 'saying' and bring that into the light of God's truth and the Holy Spirit. But here we are speaking about how we move into our birthright in our daily walk with Jesus.

Those provisos do not nullify John 10:4 but rather give us confidence in hearing. Our experience with many clients is that God will specifically answer specific questions. Especially when a person is first moving into this truth, they may ask Him for some revelation and pause to listen. When we ask what they heard, the person may say, "Nothing." In the majority of times, when pressed, they will then mention a fleeting thought, impression or picture which they had dismissed, hence their "nothing".

This is where we would explain that there are three parts to what we hear from God. One is the revelation; the second is the interpretation; and the third is the application. In our experience, hearing from God tends to be a conversation. Of course, it is possible for God to respond straight away with the revelation, interpretation and application in full, but frequently He does not do so but chats with us about those until we have understood what He wants to say. I have seen this happen so often that I wonder if, knowing that if He told us everything we would run off and get on with it, He draws the conversation out because He likes our company.[27]

So, on hearing their "nothing", we would encourage them to ask God questions about their fleeting revelation; for example, what does it

---

[27] Zephaniah 3:17 does say He delights in us – amazing!

mean? The Holy Spirit will usually respond and the conversation continues, much to the client's delight and encouragement.

When the "nothing" is accurate, they actually did not receive even a fleeting impression etc., we encourage the client to ask God to show them what is in the way of their hearing. Scripture is clear that God wants to communicate with His people, and that it is our birthright to hear Him, so if communication is not taking place, something must be in the way. In our experience with hundreds of clients over the years, on all occasions this has happened God has revealed what was in the way. His silence was His way of drawing the client's attention to the block so that it could be removed.

We know from Isaiah 55:8.9 that God's thoughts and ways are beyond ours. So a fundamental principle in our relationship with God is that we have to allow Him to be God. We must avoid the temptation to reject anything that does not make sense to us. That would be to reduce Him to less than us, and to exalt ourselves into being His judge. That is very much the way of the enemy and of our reason-exalting world but should be anathema to one who recognises Jesus as Lord and Almighty God. Humility helps us hear Him.

Our birthright of hearing God is vital to our following the Holy Spirit as He leads us into the truth. We do not have to rely upon vague impressions but we can ask Him specific questions and receive His specific answers.

Jesus, our example

> *Blessed are those who hunger and thirst for righteousness, for they will be filled.*
>
> *Matthew 5:6.*

Salvation imparts Jesus' righteousness to us. Here Jesus promises that if we really focus and desire to live out His righteousness in our daily lives, to live like Him, as He designed us to be, He will satisfy that hunger and thirst.

> *Blessed are the pure in heart for they shall see God.*
>
> *Matthew 5:8.*

Jesus says that intimacy with God comes from being pure in heart. Salvation is outworked through God changing our heart of stone, which is the heart life moulded, into a heart of flesh, which is the heart renewed in the Spirit. He does this as we follow the Spirit.

Jesus exemplified following the Spirit. Look at His response to the Syro-Phoenician woman. From Matthew 15:21-23 it is clear that the woman followed Him and His disciples, repeatedly crying out, long enough for the disciples to become embarrassed and want Jesus to send her away. He clearly had been ignoring her. Verses 24-26 show Jesus speaking quite roughly to her in a manner quite inconsistent with His normal treatment of women, although quite consistent with the chauvinism of Jewish society at that time.

We could read this incident and conclude that it is good to make 'outsiders' wait. Or we could see it as Jesus encouraging us into persistent intercession. Were either of these the reason Jesus dealt with this lady in this way? I would suggest not, because Jesus explained elsewhere the life choice that governed how He dealt with people. In John 5:19 He said, "The Son ... can only do what he sees his father doing," and in verse 30, "I judge only as I hear." He adds in John 5:49, "...for I did not speak of my own accord, but the father who sent me commanded me what to say and how to say it." In other words, Jesus dealt with this lady as the Father wanted. When she started calling out, we can assume Jesus asked the Spirit what to do and as a result ignored her. Similarly, we can assume that when the Spirit did tell Him to speak, He also told Him what to say and how to say it. How did Jesus know? He knew by being closely attuned to the leading of the Spirit.

That is how Jesus followed the Spirit. That is how *we* follow the Spirit.

Exercise

To answer or ignore as you wish.

1) What is your belief about the Bible's authority and purpose?
2) Are there any areas where you interpret the Bible in the light of your culture?
3) If so, how do those help you live like Jesus and demonstrate His Kingdom in your circle of influence?
4) Do you expect to hear God speaking to you in the way described in this chapter? If not, would you like to do so?
5) What would you find difficult about doing so?

6) Would you talk to Jesus about that, following the guidelines in this chapter?

Aide memoire

- We are speaking with our loving Father, Almighty God, so focus on Him.
- Tune out other voices (i.e. distractions): environmental, physical, emotional.
- Ask the Holy Spirit if there is any sin coming between you and deal with any He shows.
- Bind other voices however you normally do, for example, "I bind anything fleshly or soulish within me, and in the name and authority of Jesus Christ bind any spirit which would interfere with my hearing God clearly."
- Ask a specific question.
- Listen for the reply – it may be a sense, feeling, picture, impression etc.
- If there is nothing, ask what is preventing you hearing.
- If there is something but you don't understand its significance, ask Him what it means.
- Continue the conversation until you have His answer.

CHAPTER SIX

A Biblical, Not Western, Approach

We can liken a person to a house which has foundations, walls and a roof.

The 'foundations' to a person are their history from the preceding generations. Their 'walls' are cognitions and emotions. Their 'roof' is that they are spiritual beings.

Foundations

Walls are intrinsically influenced by the foundations, which is why a builder spends such care in ensuring the foundations are level. I built Helen a three-roomed cabin 30 feet long, 15 wide and 20 to the top of the eaves. Due to the slope of the site, the tongue and groove logs were laid on 20+ brick piers. The design allowed for a tolerance of only 3mm in their level. Despite my best efforts, the tolerances were slightly out. This meant that the higher the walls rose, the harder it was to fit the tongues in the grooves.

A person's foundation is their history which is laid before they are born but will influence their growth. We are familiar with that in terms of genes influencing our personality but there's also a spiritual aspect. In Exodus 20:6 God says the blessing of obedience goes to a thousand generations and the curse of disobedience to three or four. This verse tells us three things:

- It is a principle that the lifestyle of each generation has an effect on successive generations.
- Where the effects are positive, God is quite happy for that to continue indefinitely.
- Where the effects are negative, God sets a limit.

Exercise

1) Can you identify positive family traits that have been advantageous to your family line?
2) Can you identify negative family traits that have been disadvantageous to your family line?

Walls

Walls govern the shape of the building. The equivalent 'walls' for people are the emotions that are part of our experiences and the cognitions we form from our experiences. By cognitions we refer to beliefs but not, as a Christian might initially anticipate, beliefs in terms of doctrine. Rather we mean those beliefs which we have developed over time about ourselves, life and others.

The walls of emotions and cognitions are not separate brick walls. It's not as if you have a wall of cognitions and a separate wall of emotions. These are more like the walls of a cob house. Cob walls are actually mud, straw and stone intermingled. Similarly, our emotions and cognitions are intertwined. We will look further at how cognitions and emotions intertwine but before that let us complete our house.

Roof

As we have seen, God made us in His image and He is a spiritual being. It is our creation as spiritual beings and our sharing His spiritual life that distinguishes us from animals. God's intention was that we would continue in relationship with Him but unfortunately man chose to exercise his free will to rebel against God. Putting our will before God's is the root of sin and necessarily creates a rift between God and man. We chose to separate from Him. In so doing we became disconnected from God's Spirit who is the source of all life. That rift separates us from life, and the absence of life is death. Physical death happens to all of us after a number of years, but spiritual death occurred immediately to Adam and

Eve and all their descendants. The flow of spiritual life ceased and we became spiritually dead. Yet we are still, to a greater or lesser extent, spiritually aware, realising that 'something is missing'. All have an inner emptiness and longing. In the words of Blaise Pascal:

> ...what else does this craving, and this helplessness, proclaim but that there was once in man a true happiness, of which all that now remains is the empty print and trace? This he tries in vain to fill with everything around him, seeking in things that are not there the help he cannot find in those that are, though none can help, since this infinite abyss can be filled only with an infinite and immutable object; in other words, by God himself.[28]

Only reconnection with the Spirit of God can bring real fulfilment. The God-shaped hole at our core can only properly be filled by the One whose space it is. Until then, we seek to fill that hole, find purpose and value, in all sorts of substitutes. Inevitably, born under the dominion of darkness, some of those substitutes enable the enemy to oppress us. We live, as it were, under his covering; he becomes our roof.

Exercise

1) Have you recognised your God-shaped hole and, if so, with what do you try to fill it?
2) If with God, is that God alone or God plus (additions could be career, marriage, children, ministry etc.)?

We will look in greater detail at our foundations, walls and roof – for brevity let's call them our four heart areas – but let us first consider two fundamentally different approaches to how we repair our house when we notice a problem.

The Western approach to house repair

Western culture, and in particular the education system, is based on our Greek intellectual heritage which is fundamentally rational and analytical. Many a heart will sink at the recollection of endless fruitless discussions as to the difference between body, soul and spirit. Our cultural paradigm is to see those as different and to analyse and classify.

---

[28] Blaise Pascal; *Pensées;* 'A Defence of Christian Religion'.

In many areas there are great benefits from an analytical approach but there are also disadvantages if it is the only approach used. One from which the Church and many Christians have suffered is the tendency to approach lifestyle problems analytically.

Let us imagine a person with problems; they need a house repair.

To the Western mind the first step is to analyse, what is the source of the problem? As we talk it may be that the problem seems to flow from incorrect or unscriptural cognitions. Bible study, conference or sermon may be recommended and may lead the person to adopt more scriptural cognitions in the hope that this will solve the problem. However, as we will see, in absence of a miracle it will take six weeks or so before the new cognition is established. If in that period the person has an experience that resonates with the earlier experience which led to or reinforced the original cognition, that resonance with its emotional content will stimulate the old cognitions. The new cognitions may well be 'washed away'.

To illustrate: when I was thirteen my dressing table had a three-part mirror which enabled you to see each profile as well as full face. I caught a glimpse of my profile and was painfully shocked to realise that I was ugly. Many years later, as a Christian, I read scriptures which told me that I was fearfully and wonderfully made and I tried to live those out, but usually something would happen to reinforce the pain of being ugly. It was not until I experienced the love of the most beautiful woman in the world, and heard that some of her friends were jealous because they had wanted to marry me, that the comfort of that love removed the impediment to my believing the scripture.

Back to our house repair. From conversation it may have become clear that the person's problem lies with an emotional pain, need or deficit. So the person was encouraged to receive prayer or ministry for the wounding. Our God being loving, they may have a very real experience of God meeting the pain or other distress with very real comfort. However, if the cognitions formed from the original experience that resulted in the pain, need or deficit remain intact, they will be influential in any subsequent resonating experience. The new comfort may be overwhelmed.

To illustrate[29]: to all appearances Mary was an attractive and intelligent lady in her twenties but she had experienced great rejection. The time came when she took her rejection to Jesus and experienced prayer ministers who encouraged her to wait with open hands before the Lord. He met her in a wonderful way, giving her a real sense of His acceptance and love. Mary was buoyed by that for some time. One Sunday she greeted her vicar as he was walking past. His mind was elsewhere and he did not notice her greeting. Immediately the rejection cognitions clicked in and she was back in the pain of rejection. Mary went through this cycle of 'pain → meeting Jesus → renewed pain' repeatedly.

Back to our house repair. Where our person who needs a house repair has tried believing the truth and then tried receiving prayer (not necessarily in that order) but the problem persists, the person and those helping him may conclude that the problem must be spiritual. There must be spiritual oppression from which the person needs to be delivered. He or she may go to a deliverance minister or ministry and they may well receive deliverance. However, Ephesians 6 tells us there is a continual spiritual battle. As we will see, family traits, emotional reactions and cognitions that are sinful are an open door to enemy oppression. If these are not dealt with at the same time as the deliverance, at best the door will easily be reopened to further infestation.

To illustrate: Alfie had been orphaned and received effective deliverance from an orphan spirit. He began to live in the freedom of being God's son but his cognitions and emotional pain were not ministered into. As Alfie continued to live in those, they created fresh landing strips for the enemy and when he came to us, he was again oppressed.

This analytical approach tends to deal with only one aspect of the 'house' and is possibly one of the reasons for the very common experience where a person has a meaningful conference, prayer experience or deliverance but it does not last. The person may then be looking for the next conference, prayer method or 'man of power for the hour' to finally solve the problem. They may ride on that expensive and time-consuming merry-go-round for some time. Or, they may conclude in the end that

---

[29] I should make clear that those illustrations which do not come from my own story are what is known in the profession as from 'hip-pocket clients', real life but non-identifiable experiences. I name them for your ease in reading.

nothing seems to work and so stop looking for 'an answer'; they may settle for life less than the abundance Jesus promised; they may become 'realistic', having lost their 'youthful enthusiasm' and may see this as the 'cross' they have to bear.

Exercise

1) Are you aware of any area of your house that still needs repair?
2) Can you identify with any of these cycles of repairs that seem permanent but prove to be temporary? If so, in what areas?

Biblical house repair

There is another way, a hope-filled way. We understand that in contrast to the Greek, the way the Hebrews understood things (which is the perspective of scripture) was synthetic. This can be understood by taking a synthetic approach to the question of describing body, soul and spirit. Imagine furniture within a room which has windows in three separate walls. One window represents body, another soul and another spirit. Whichever window we look through, we will always see the same furniture but it will look different depending upon which window it is. An accurate description of the furniture would need us to look through every window. One particular window may not add much but omitting one may mean we miss some important aspect of the furniture.

In our ministry we adopt this approach when helping clients. We encourage them to look at the problem from each aspect. Is there a foundational family trait which is sinful? Are there non-godly cognitions that need to become godly? Are there emotions which need to be expressed appropriately and for which the client needs to discover Christ's comfort and perspective? Is there a landing strip for the enemy which needs to be recovered for Christ? The Holy Spirit leads the client through each of these areas as seems relevant to Him. He leads the client to replacement truths and blessings. As the client lives those, the client will experience lasting freedom and transformation. Many clients have dismounted from their analytically inspired merry-go-rounds – *hallelujah!*

Well done, good and faithful servant!

Exercise

1) Would you describe your approach to house repair as analytic or synthetic?
2) Why do you use that approach?

CHAPTER SEVEN

Belief Expectation Cycle

The cycle explained

The Belief Expectation Cycle is a significant mechanism God has implanted within each of us to enable us to learn. It begins with an experience leading to a belief, which leads to an expectation, which leads to behaviour, which leads to another experience, which repeats or avoids the original experience and therefore reinforces the belief.

Please notice that by belief we are not referring to Christian doctrine or practice but to cognition.

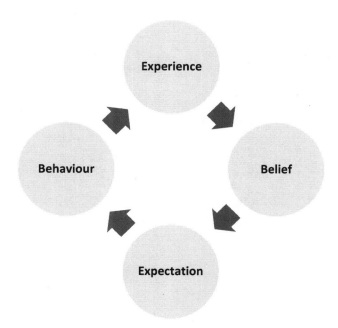

We learn because the cycle reinforces itself. One of the earliest experiences common to most of us is heat, perhaps from a fire or a radiator. As a babe we will have been told by our carer not to touch as "it is hot and hot hurts". We were given the belief "hot hurts". Our expectation was to be hurt if we touched the hot thing and not to be hurt if we didn't. If our behaviour was not to touch, we would have not been hurt, which will have reinforced the belief. If at some point we did touch and experienced the hurt of the heat, that would really have reinforced the belief!

Where the beliefs are formed without reference to God, they can be called non-godly beliefs. Some use the term *ungodly* beliefs but to us that is an overly negative term so we prefer *non*-godly. This more accurately describes their nature in that they are formed without any specific reference to God.

The non-godly belief is based on the fact of our experience, and therefore is true to life. Some such beliefs are valid and helpful, e.g. heat can hurt; too close to the edge is dangerous; and many others that we each will have formed from our unique experience.

However, this world is the dominion of darkness and ruled by Satan so there is much in life that runs counter to God and His perspective. Therefore, we each hold non-godly beliefs that are true to life but can actually be lies from God's perspective. Examples could be 'number one first', 'be successful', 'what will be will be', and many others that we each will have formed from our unique experience.

Exercise

1) What helpful non-godly beliefs come to mind?
2) What unhelpful non-godly beliefs come to mind?

Our operating system

Life can be described as a series of experiences from which we form cognitions proportionately strong according to the emotional impact of the experience. As very young children we are totally dependent on our caregivers for everything: food, drink, clothing, accommodation, security, sense of value, worth, identity, to name a few. We subconsciously build up cognitions about our carers, ourselves, others, life, God – cognitions which work to keep us 'safe' and emotionally secure in our particular environment. Any early child development specialist would agree that key aspects of a child's relationship to the world are the answers the child forms to questions such as, is the world a safe place? Is it a good place? Am I lovable? Am I valued? The most lasting answers are all decided subconsciously based on our interactions with caregivers.

These are the fundamental cognitions, reinforced and proven by our life, and so they become the foundational truths for how we choose to live. In this sense they can be fairly likened to the operating system of a computer. The operating system runs automatically in the background and enables a computer to run many varied programmes known as software. Similarly, this system of cognitions can be said to be our operating system, running automatically in our subconscious and enabling our brain, our human computer, to function in many different ways. We each have our own unique operating system.

An example of the ongoing effect of our operating system can be seen from an incident that occurred in the early months of my becoming a Christian. I was invited to a meeting in a fellow student's house. I underestimated the time it would take me to walk there and arrived a few minutes late. I was new to the group and was too scared to go in late by myself. I waited to see if anyone else would arrive because then I would be able to go in with them and, hopefully, they would be the centre of attention. No-one arrived so I went back to my room. Most would be shy about entering a new group on their own – but 'scared'?

That was an extreme reaction. It was only later that I discovered that an early traumatic experience had led to my cognition that it is not safe to be singled out. So aged twenty I expected if I went in late, I would become the centre of attention. According to my operating system, that would not be safe. So my behaviour was to go home. That was the sensible thing to do; it kept me safe. My operating system had kept me safe and, by so doing, reinforced my initial belief!

The important point to note is that although my returning home was a conscious act, it was inspired by a cognition operating in my subconscious – one of which I was entirely unaware. My operating system laid down the parameters within which I perceived my situation and chose my action. When we think of conditioning, our thoughts turn to Pavlov and his dogs, to repressive regimes, to victims of torture; but in a very real sense we have each been conditioned by our upbringing. The important difference is that our conditioning, our operating system, was not imposed by an outside agency. We chose it ourselves over time as being the best way of surviving and thriving in our environment. It is our most fundamental 'good'.

Now we know that if your computer is using an old operating system and you bought the latest version of a game, you would not be able to play it successfully because the game has been designed to run on the current version of the operating system. If you complained to the store that the game didn't work, their first question would be to ask what operating system your computer ran on. When you told them and they recognised that it was an outdated one, they would not accept the game was at fault. You would have three choices. You could continue to play the old version that runs well on your system and try to give the new game back and get a refund (unlikely, because you have used it!) You could play the new game on your system and put up with its poor performance. You could update your operating system. Most who could afford the update would say that the third choice is what in my navy days we would call a BGO, a 'blinding glimpse of the obvious'!

As we grow, we move out from our natal family into school and then society, which have different values, routines etc. from our family home. These differences, new software, lead to increasing conflict with our operating system. It was formed and has been running for years in our subconscious. We are not aware of it so do not realise one way of resolving the conflict would be to update our operating system. That is not an alternative, so our focus can only be on trying to adapt the 'software' to work with our operating system. These 'workarounds' take energy and effort which can be minimised by choosing to live in 'software' environments appropriate to our operating system. We tend to live within our comfort zone, but even so, the stresses increase as we grow older, gain more responsibilities at work and home, have children who become teenagers and possibly signed-up members of the boomerang generation. The energy required for more 'workarounds' plus the increased stresses is a combination that can lead to a host of unpleasant consequences including breakdown or blow-up in relationships and health.

A person who becomes a Christian can experience additional real difficulties in seeking to live in integrity. Christian software has been created and demonstrated by Jesus, so scope for adapting it is minimised. We just have to get this software to work somehow, not least because we are surrounded by people for whom it does seem to work well!

Perhaps 2 Corinthians 5:17, where Paul says becoming a Christian is becoming a new creation, solves the problem? It would if, to use our terminology, Paul meant becoming a Christian included receiving a complete update of one's operating system. It's a pity then that when Paul said that becoming a Christian is becoming "a new creation" he was talking about being delivered from the dominion of darkness and transferred into the Kingdom of God's beloved son by being reborn of the Spirit. The individual becomes spiritually alive whereas previously they were dead in their sin. When I became a Christian, my physical being did not change and nor did my neurological being. So when you become a Christian, you do not suddenly have a new operating system implanted in place of the one you formed and used so effectively beforehand. You continue to live by the old operating system. The new software, Christianity, conflicts in many ways.

Exercise

1) As you look back over the various changing environments into which you have grown, what areas of conflict have you experienced between those and the environment of your family of origin?
2) How do you think understanding your operating system would have helped you in those conflicts?

Mind the gap

Most people are aware of a gap between their principles and how they actually live. For Christians who seek to imitate Christ, there can seem to be not just a gap but a chasm between their daily lifestyle and the lifestyle scripture endorses. The majority will try very hard to bridge this gap. Some will be discouraged by continued failure and may give up their faith altogether, or resign themselves to church attendance and a Christianised secularity. Others may keep working hard to appear to have bridged the gap, all the time hoping others do not see just how broad the gap is. Some of these will keep pressing on but others will blow up or burn out with the effort.

I have experience of how this works in different settings. When in a conservative evangelical, Bible-believing setting which had a clear understanding of how a Christian witnessed, prayed, lived, it was very easy to live by the rules whilst lacking the intimacy from which those 'rules' were meant to flow. In this period of my life I would often say to a non-Christian that being a Christian was not following a religion of rules but was having a relationship, yet in my heart of hearts I knew I was not enjoying the depth of relationship with Jesus which I held to be the essence of Christianity. Indeed, it was that discrepancy that fuelled my hunger and led me onto the long journey out of which I am writing this book.

At another stage in my Christian journey there were times when I lived with real tension between what I believed about God's ability and my experience, in which He seemed not to be answering prayer or healing. I was leading in charismatic house churches where there was a strong belief in the power of the Holy Spirit, in declaring the truth and in faith demonstrated by a positive confession. In that context it was difficult to be honest about the tension e.g. when healing did not occur. When I did express that tension, I was warned that doing so was a negative confession and hindered healing. Whilst I hold onto my belief in a God who can and does at times work miraculously (I have seen Him do so), He had to be very patient with me until I finally learnt that maturity is not hiding the gap behind a 'front' of faith. Rather it is being honest with Him, and others, about the gap and asking Him for the 'one step at a time' which enables me to narrow the gap.

By the way, one step after another is called walking. Before Jesus' followers were called Christians, they were known as 'followers of the Way'. As we walk one step at a time with the Way, who is Truth, we experience His Life.

Exercise

1) Are you aware of a gap?
2) If you are, how are you coping with it?
3) Does your environment encourage honesty about your gaps? If not, what could you do to help bring about more honesty?

Deferred destruction

In John 17 Jesus did not pray that we would be taken out of the world but rather that God would keep us safe from the evil one. In Ephesians 6 Paul makes it very clear that we are involved in a spiritual battle. Our enemy should not overawe us but nor should we underestimate him. One of his more successful tactics throughout history has been that of deferred destruction. Perhaps he is able to identify Christians who are gifted and called to leadership, but it is undoubtedly the case that there are too many leaders who fall at the point in their ministry where their doing so not only damages themselves and their family but also damages many other Christians and a significant work for the Kingdom of God. Yet hindsight shows in many cases the cause of their fall was something that had been around for many years and which the enemy could have used at any time to bring them down. It seems he prefers to defer until many can be damaged.

It is emotionally, spiritually and physically draining to hide the gap, or to keep trying to live as if there is no gap. The enemy waits until that drain has rendered the Christian susceptible to temptation and then strikes. This is not a case where 'practice makes perfect' but rather one where struggle collapses into surrender.

When I say "to hide the gap, or to keep trying to live as if there is no gap" please do not understand me to be saying that the Christian intends to deceive. It is more a case of self-deception through ignorance of the operating system. Not understanding 'how we tick', nor that there is an area of our operating system which is working against our professed and desired lifestyle, we just keep trying. We may be aware of inconsistencies but not have the knowledge or tools to change. In mechanical terms, we won't solve the problem of our car pulling to one side by inflating the tyres if the tracking is out. But if we do not know about the tracking system, that may seem to be all we can do.

A significant part of our calling is to enable people to live in integrity through the process of learning how their inner being works, and how to co-operate with the Holy Spirit to update their operating system and so, by successive simple steps, to live in integrity, true to their calling. We see the broken-hearted, whatever the source of their pain, become brave-hearted.

Exercise

Please pause to pray for those who have fallen prey to deferred destruction, their families, churches and others affected – that there would be forgiveness, healing and they would resist the temptation to return to ministry before finding the roots of the access point(s).

Updating

This is the crux. As we said, our operating system operates subconsciously for many years and so very few people outside of psychotherapeutic circles are aware that they have an operating system.

Where a Christian does not even understand that he has an operating system, he is unable to address the real seat of the problem, which is the need for the operating system to be updated.

Before Jesus left His disciples, He told them that it was better for them that He did so because then He would be able to send them the Holy Spirit who would guide them into all truth. It is the truth that would set them free. The Psalmist prayed in Psalm 139:23, "Search me, O God, and know my heart; test me and know my anxious thoughts. See if there is any offensive way in me, and lead me in the way everlasting." "Offensive" is English for the Hebrew *rasah*, a legal term for breaking the law. God clearly wants truth in our inward parts. Another way of expressing this is to say that part of the Holy Spirit's role is to enable us to see where there is a discrepancy between living as a Christian and living in accordance with our operating system and then to enable us to 'update' the latter so that we can live in integrity.

A reader could be excused for thinking, "This is just another set of complicated activity. I've got to be aware of what I think and say and feel; bring that to the Spirit; become aware of and implement the updates He gives. My life is busy enough without taking on this burden. I prefer a simple Christianity."

I agree and am not suggesting a new set of principles to apply. We saw earlier that that is Pharisee-ism. Jesus said, "I am the Way," and I do suggest there are four different ways of walking with The Way.

If we say that being a person is owning and driving a car then we could say becoming a Christian is inviting Jesus into our car. We could be the driver and let Him ride in the back, largely ignoring Him apart from occasional interaction. Or we could let Him sit in the front and talk more with Him, but we are still in the driver's seat. Both of these could be Christianised secularity i.e. there may be no substantial difference between my life and that of my secular neighbour beyond the fact that he is a golfer and spends his Sundays on the golf course and I am a Christian who spends my Sunday in church. Of course, if you press us, we will both talk about our interest, but we will be careful not to bore you with it, perhaps the Christian being more circumspect than the golfer!

Another two ways would be where we invite Jesus to drive the car. Now we go where He wants. Where do we sit? We could sit in the back and busy ourselves with useful things, occasionally relating to Jesus, especially whenever He relates to us, but otherwise making the most of our time. In other words, we treat Jesus like our chauffeur. Or we could sit alongside Jesus and chat with Him about where He is taking us and why, and what He wants us to do there; in the meantime enjoying the journey with Him, perhaps periods of shared silence, or of deep intimacy, or of chatting about what we see on our journey.

We would all prefer the latter but recognise, I'm sure, that at various times we have been in each configuration. We change seats, sometimes as often as in a child's game of musical chairs. Events, people, our operating system are the music prompting the changes. We need to make a conscious daily effort to relate to Jesus as He drives. Is this why Paul pummelled his body; exhorted us to be filled and continually be being filled with the Spirit; to rejoice always, pray continually, give thanks in all circumstances?

Updating our operating system is not an add-on to an already busy life. It is listening to the Spirit as He leads us through our walk through each day. It is responding to His promptings: "Encourage this one, help that one, pray for another, love those around by speaking and demonstrating the Kingdom as Jesus did." Be Jesus to your neighbour. As we seek to walk in the Way, we will soon be aware of difficulties external and internal. The Spirit will help us with both. My hope is that understanding how we function will help us to be more intimate with Jesus, more who we were designed to be, walking increasingly into our destiny so that we each have incredibly magnificent crowns to lay at Jesus' feet and He is overwhelmed with joy as He sees the fruit of the travail of His soul in and through our lives.

Not an added burden but an aide to fulfilled desire.

We will look later at the practical ways in which the Holy Spirit helps us bring this about but first let us look in more detail at our four heart areas to see how our operating system is formed and works.

Exercise

1) How sensitive are you to the Spirit's promptings to update an area of your operating system?
2) Which seating configuration do you and Jesus occupy most often?
3) In which situations do you change chairs in a way with which He is not happy? If not sure, perhaps you could ask Him.
4) Would you like to ask Him what alterations, if any, He would like you to make?

CHAPTER EIGHT

First Heart Area: Foundations

We saw that positive and negative spiritual effects run down our family line and that God intends the negative to be limited to three or four generations. However, we know that sin can only be dealt with by being brought to the cross so, of course, if no-one during those three or four generations brings that sin to the cross, the fourth generation becomes another first one. The consequence will carry on down the line.

Scripture speaks of these ongoing effects in terms of the blessing of obedience and the curse of disobedience. Some might wrongly interpret the "curse of disobedience" as meaning that we have a God who sees us sinning and responds by seeking to hurt our children. In contrast, we understand blessing and curse to be the outworking of the fundamental life principle that actions have inevitable consequences across the generations. Good consequences are blessings and bad ones are curses. To illustrate the latter: if I were to defy the law of gravity by jumping off the roof of a house, when I landed I would suffer the curse of gravity, i.e. its consequence. Let's say I'm fortunate and only break a leg. Unlike breaking the law of gravity, which is purely physical and has physical effects, God's law is spiritual and, as we have seen, has spiritual effects. If sin in a family is not brought to the cross, the bad consequence (or curse) is that it goes down to the next generation. Some people refer to this as the resultant curse of generational sin but that is rather off-putting terminology so we refer to 'the ongoing consequences of family history' or 'family traits'.

A way of understanding this effect is to think of a game of bowls. First the small bowl, the jack, is bowled and then the aim is to get your larger two bowls as close to the jack as possible. The closest wins. Each large bowl has a weight in it which creates a bias so that it won't roll straight but will deviate according to the bias. Similarly, what we are talking about here is the way that sin patterns can be passed down by previous generations. The next generation is, as it were, set up to have certain sin reactions to certain situations. You can see these patterns of behaviour going down the generations. Examples could be patterns of adultery, of passivity, of control, of emotional distance and many more. One pattern in my family line is that both my grandfathers were piece-workers i.e. they were paid for each piece of good work they produced. As a result, working well and fast were high values. Good in themselves, these qualities became harmful idols when they were insisted upon inappropriately. In my case they led to workaholism.

You may be able to look into your family and see patterns of behaviour which do not align with the way Jesus would want us to behave. We are all affected to some extent so when we are born, we do not inherit sound foundations. This means, continuing the illustration of a house, as we build the house (which is our life) we are building with a particular propensity for particular sin reactions.

Exercise

1) What adverse traits did you notice if you did the exercise in the foundations section on page 55?

2) Draw a family tree going back into each of your parental lines as far as you have knowledge including, where possible, number of children, occupation, date and cause of death. Are there any patterns, e.g. early death, particular illnesses, miscarriage, divorce, etc.?

3) Do you see any of the behaviours in the column below in your family line, in your past or current experience? (You might make three further columns – 'family line', 'my past', 'my current' – and mark where you see them.)

Adultery, pornography
Anxiety, panic attacks
Chemical and behavioural addictions
Depression, mental illness
Divorce
Eating disorders
Financial instability, poverty, debt
Gambling
Illegitimacy
Infertility and barrenness
Infirmities

Well done, good and faithful servant!

Lying, cheating, stealing
Miscarriages or abortions
Neglect
Emotional, physical and/or verbal abuse
Secret societies e.g. Masons
Sexual abuse
Sexual immorality
Suicide
Anger, rage
Violence or murder
Witchcraft/occult

CHAPTER NINE

Second Heart Area: Cognitions

We have seen that as we experience life we build up a whole system of beliefs about life, ourselves and others, including God, and these become our operating system by which we seek to live safely.

These beliefs are built up over time so we can identify three sets of beliefs created at differing stages of our physical growth. Traditionally it was thought that life began when we were born but it is now well established that a foetus is aware of its mother and develops cognitions within the womb. We have a lovely example of this. One of our sons-in-law is a keen drummer and worshipper. Before our granddaughter was born, her dad would beatbox and sing worship songs to her through Mummy's tummy, one song in particular. When she was born, she recognised that song. She had learnt it within the womb. These early cognitions are learnt by instinct or intuition.

At a later date, usually by about two years of age, we learn to speak and develop the ability to learn through perception. A lovely game we played with our children illustrates this. Before your child has developed perception, you can play 'hide the toy'. You show the toy to your child and they see it. While they are still watching, you place the toy under the rug and the child has no idea where the toy is. Later on, you can play the same game and now your child knows that the toy is under the rug. Your little one has developed perception!

A few years later, usually by age seven, your child will have developed the ability to reason and will now form cognitions by reason.

So each of us has an operating system which includes three sorts of cognitions.

- Ones that 'make sense' and which we can express, because they were formed when we were rational and had language.
- Other cognitions which we can express, because they were formed after we had language, but they don't 'make sense',

because these were formed before we developed reason. We experience this in our ministry when we ask a client a question and we can see from their body language that they have a response but they say something like "nothing is happening". When we ask them what is in the way of their saying what is actually going on, they express reluctance because "it doesn't make sense". When encouraged not to allow reason a veto, they are able to express their cognition.

- Finally, there are cognitions which were formed before we had reason and therefore they don't 'make sense', and also before we had language and so we have difficulty in expressing them in words. Secular therapists will use techniques such as hypnotherapy, EMDR therapy for trauma, and others to try to help the client gain some awareness of these cognitions. Many Christians will have hesitations about therapies that open one's mind to another's direct influence. There may be times where some may find these helpful, but our experience is that the Holy Spirit who was present when the cognitions were laid down is very happy to reveal them, as His role is to lead us into all truth.

Exercise

1) If this understanding is new to you, please take some time to meditate upon it with Jesus to see how He wants you to address it.
2) Upon which of the three sets of cognitions do you place most weight?
3) Are there areas or subjects where you would dismiss a prompting because "it does not make sense"?

There are four other aspects of cognitions which significantly affect how we live and so recognising them can be helpful. Let's look at these now.

Weight

Our society places a high value on reason, some would even say it is one of our idols. When I, a lawyer, married Helen, a health visitor, she actually earned more than I did as we were both at the start of our careers but we quite rightly expected that as we progressed my career would lead to greater remuneration and status than hers. If our society placed a higher value on compassion than reason, that would not have been a reasonable expectation.

One outworking of this far greater weight on the rational is that in many instances the other two sets of cognitions are ignored. This can be particularly true for men. In our marriage enrichment ministry we have frequently observed that a source of disagreement in marriage lies in men's tendency to rely almost exclusively on rationality whereas women are happy to supplement that with perception and intuition. Sometimes where a husband and wife disagree about some decision, the man will ask his wife for the reason behind her preference. She may not be able to satisfy him, perhaps because her preference is based on intuition or perception more than reason. If he dismisses or overrides her because she can't make a good argument for her preference, their relationship may be running into danger. Sadly, the men most likely to adopt this behaviour are the 'successful' as their success may well flow from, and reinforce the importance of, rationality.

It's only fair to mention that in some relationships the wife can be the spouse who esteems reason more than intuition or perception.

Proverbs 22:6 says, "Train a child in the way he should go, and when he is old he will not turn from it." There is a saying, attributed to Aristotle and to the Jesuits, "Give me a boy until he is seven and I will give you the man." This principle was utilised when Turks kidnapped young Christian boys, forced them to convert to Islam and trained them to be Janissaries, an elite force that fought against Christians; when Hitler indoctrinated young children in the Hitler Jugend to create loyal cadres; when communist regimes took the young into groups such as Komosol.

From what we have seen about our cognitions there are three very important points to read, learn and inwardly digest, as the saying goes:

- Our core beliefs are laid down in the earliest years, well before the age of seven.
- Of the three sets of beliefs, the pre-language and pre-reason are the most influential.
- If we do buy into society's idolisation of reason and make that our litmus test, we will not recognise the majority of our most important cognitions.

Well done, good and faithful servant!

Exercise

1) To what extent, or in what areas, do you buy into society's idolisation of reason?
2) How would your repenting of that idol alter your relationships?

Neurology

We are probably all aware that a thought is a chemical reaction which takes place between synapses in the brain. Neurologists tell us that for a thought to become a habit it needs to be repeated for about six weeks.

Now, of course it is possible for God to work miraculously. One of my first answers to prayer after becoming a Christian happened after I asked God "to help me stop smoking" when I had "finished the ones I bought". I used to buy in bulk as I smoked sixty-five king-sized a day. The previous year I had realised my health was being affected so had twice tried to stop but had been unsuccessful. About three weeks after that prayer, I was amazed to realise I had not been smoking for several days and had not missed it. I asked my dad for a cigarette and he refused to give me one saying, "You've stopped smoking." I had to buy one off him! The first drag was awful. God had completely taken away my desire for nicotine and replaced it with an aversion to cigarettes. In other words, He had sovereignly updated my operating system.

This was very significant because it was my first answered prayer that could not be explained away as coincidence or my effort, because after praying I had forgotten about it. Perhaps God gave me this miracle because He knew I lacked will power. Perhaps He wanted me to see His reality in such a clear way to give me confidence that He is real and quite independent of me. I don't know why He updated my operating system this way but I do know this is not His usual way. He does not want infants who are helpless unless He steps in. His desire is that we grow into mature people of God by who by constant use have trained ourselves to distinguish good from evil.[30] The process of reinforcing the godly belief over a period of six weeks helps us to grow in maturity.

---

[30] See Hebrews 5:14.

Judgement

Another understanding which has brought great relief to many is the recognition that when I form a judgement, such as "my wife is lazy", that is not simply a judgement. It is also an instruction to my brain to filter input. In other words, I am also telling my brain (1) not to pay attention to any information that runs counter to that judgement, and (2) to pay attention to information that fits in with it.

Think of an example where I spend all day working with Helen whom I judge to be lazy. She could be very industrious but have an hour for lunch. At the end of the day, when thinking about her day, I would not have noticed her industry because my brain would have filtered out that input. However, I would have noticed how long she took for lunch. My brain would have accepted that input because it fits in with my judgement. My conclusion would be a reinforcement of my judgement – yes, she is lazy.

I learnt this truth in the first year of marriage. I cannot remember what judgement I had formed about Helen (although she tells me it was that she did not tidy things away) but I clearly recall how astounded I was at the radical change in her behaviour within twenty-four hours of my breaking the judgement. Of course, she had not changed at all. (Helen tells me she had been tidying for ages before I noticed!) By breaking my judgement, I had removed the filter on my brain so I began to notice behaviour which I had previously ignored. We will look later at how to break a judgement.

Exercise

1) Draw four columns headed 'item', 'mum', 'dad', 'me' and then make rows for 'men', 'women', 'children', 'teenagers', 'family', 'job', 'money', 'sex', 'church', 'vicars/ministers' and any other item that would be helpful. Then in each column write what the person at the head of that column would say about the item on that row. For the 'me' column, try to write your pre-rebirth belief rather than what you now know scripture would say. My table would be:

Item	Mum	Dad	Me
Men	Are lazy	Provide	Must be successful

Well done, good and faithful servant!

2) Read through and notice those that are judgements (e.g. Mum's "men are lazy"). Then note any with which you agree in your gut.
3) Ask the Spirit to show you any judgements you hold and which He wants to free you from.
   (We will look later at how we become free from them.)

Non-godly to godly beliefs

Beliefs based on our pre-Christian experience we call non-godly beliefs, not in any negative sense, but because they are formed without any reference to God. This hints at the way of resolving a non-godly belief once you become aware of it.

Rather than letting the Belief Expectation Cycle begin at the point of experience, you let the cycle begin with God and His truth so they become the basis for your belief or cognition.

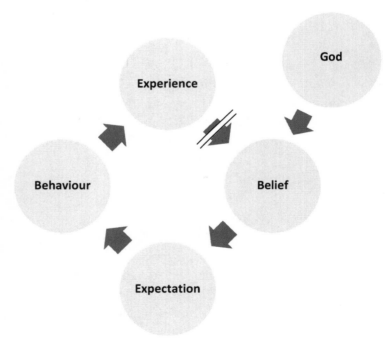

We break the cycle at the link between Experience and Belief and then start a fresh cycle from the basis of God and His truth. This will result in different beliefs, godly ones, which will lead to different expectations. Consequently, there will be different behaviour resulting in different experience. That will again reinforce the original (but this time godly) belief. The cycle is always reinforcing.

Exercise

1) Read through the table you made above and identify any non-godly beliefs with which you agree in your gut.

2) Ask the Spirit to show you any other non-godly beliefs you hold and which He wants to free you from.
   (Don't worry if none come to mind. We will look at how to identify them later.)

CHAPTER TEN

Third Heart Area: Emotion

We have seen that emotion is intertwined with cognition to form the walls of our house so let us consider emotion in more depth.

Meaning

This section will please all classicists! Emotion is derived from *emotum*, the supine of *emovere* – 'to move out', and means 'having moved out'. It is as if a classicist saw one person laughing hysterically, another being furiously angry, and a third weeping in deep grief; he recognised that the common factor in each case was that energy was being expressed, was moving out from the person, and so he described that energy as emotion. So the very name emotion signifies energy that is to be expressed.

Morality

If a visitor from outer space were to observe how we talk about emotion, he would deduce that we consider some emotion to be good and some to be bad. Sometimes I like to be mischievous and ask a client to give me an example of a bad emotion. The one that most often comes to mind is anger. The difficulty with this line of thinking is that it necessarily means that God commands us to sin because in Ephesians 4:26 He commands, "Be ... angry."[31] But God would not tell us to sin! If the client remembers that Jesus whipped the moneychangers out of the temple, His behaviour is excused as being "righteous anger".

James 1:14-15 tells us that the source of sin is evil desire: "...but each person is tempted when they are dragged away by their own evil desire and enticed. Then, after desire has conceived, it gives birth to sin; and sin, when it is full-grown, gives birth to death." God does not have any

---

[31] KJV.

evil desires. Being angry is not of itself sinful, nor is being jealous. God is described as a jealous God and we are told the Spirit yearns jealously over us. The apparent contradiction in a pure God commanding us to express 'bad' emotion is resolved by recognising that *all emotion is amoral*.

Morality is determined by the expression of the emotion, which is why Ephesians 4:26 continues, "…but sin not." From that warning it is clearly possible to be angry and not sin, as well as to be angry and sin.

Appropriate…

…is the keyword. This is vividly illustrated by a shameful incident from my early days as a father of three children with only three years and three weeks between births of the eldest and youngest. There are many blessings in having children so closely together, but it is really hard work when they are little. One night my two little girls were not settling to sleep as asked. I became very angry and put my fist through the stud bedroom wall. This scared them and later in life one had ministry to deal with the effects of this incident. Clearly, that expression of my anger was inappropriate. If I'd gone into my bedroom and expressed my anger by hitting my pillow, that would have been appropriate.

Safe expressions of emotion are:

- appropriate as to manner (hit the pillow, not the child or the wall);
- appropriate as to time (so not expressing straight away in front of the children but waiting until away from them);
- appropriate as to place (somewhere nice and private like my bedroom); and
- appropriate as to duration (not allowing the emotion to fester and affect life around us).

We can each find our ways of appropriately expressing emotion. At various times I have hit my pillow; smashed a squash ball around the squash court; screamed out loud in the privacy of my car on the motorway; thrown sticks for my dog and shouted directions to help her retrieve, though I would not have been surprised if she found my directions quite superfluous as usually she could retrieve sticks without them!

Well done, good and faithful servant!

By the way, clearly in God's eyes, whipping the temple clean was appropriate. Jesus must have heard very clear leading from the Spirit to do so!

Men

Apart from that pernicious lie told to many boys that "emotion is weakness", which leads to many husbands being emotionally illiterate and their wives lonely, men have a particular problem of which they become aware to varying degrees through adolescence. As little boys they may have been quite free in expressing their emotion but as they grow into manhood even the weakest become aware of their physical strength. They realise that they could do real damage if, as men, they were to express their emotion as freely as when they were boys. They can become very wary of strong emotion and err on the side of stifling it. Parents could help their adolescent children here by encouraging them to express their emotion appropriately. We had trees in our garden. Helen encouraged our son to hit a stick against the trees or, even more satisfyingly, against a dustbin lid. He found these to be particularly useful ways of handling, for example, the frustration of exam revision.

Emotion/soul akin to pain/body

Leprosy is a terrible disease which can affect the sensory, peripheral, motor and autonomic nerves. When the sensory nerves are damaged, they cannot register pain. This leaves the extremities of hands and feet vulnerable to burns and injuries that can result in the loss of fingers, toes, hands and feet. Whilst we do not like pain, we do recognise the value of pain to the body. If when walking you felt a stone in your shoe, your immediate response would be to remove it as soon as possible. You know that if you do not do so you will develop a blister. If you do not respond to that pain it may well become infected. If you do not respond to the pain of the infection you could develop gangrene leading to the loss of a limb or even death. I'm pretty confident that you do not know anyone who died because they picked up a stone in their shoe!

Yet that is exactly what we frequently do with emotion. One of the key values of emotion to our well-being is that it plays the same role to our souls as pain does to our body. Let me immediately say that I am not using 'soul' as a religious word but rather referring to our non-corporeal being. A technical word might well be *psyche*. Pain warns us something

82

is adversely affecting our body. Likewise, emotion tells us that something is affecting our soul. For our well-being we need to develop an emotional awareness as sensitive as our peripheral nerves are to pain. Clearly pleasant emotions are no more of a cause of concern than would be bathing hot feet in cool water. Unpleasant emotions are akin to a stone in the shoe and should receive our early if not immediate attention. Unfortunately, many of us have not developed the skills to be emotionally self-aware. For such there can be disastrous consequences on our health and relationships.

A one-tap system

We have seen that there are not good and bad emotions. If there were, that would be a two-tap system. Just as you can turn off the hot tap when it is scalding but keep the cold flowing, so we would be able to turn off a 'bad' emotion such as fury but keep flowing a 'good' emotion such as happiness. As all emotion is amoral, it is actually a one-tap system. If we choose to restrict the flow of emotion we consider to be bad, that restriction necessarily impedes the flow of emotion we consider to be good. This can have several effects.

On a personal basis, failure to freely and appropriately express emotion leads to it being bottled up somewhere in our bodies. We all carry our stress in a particular part of our body. That failure to express emotion can lead to physical illness. In 1997 the World Health Organisation published that 20% of illnesses are psychosomatic. A GP told me a little while ago that over 85% of his patients present with symptoms that are psychosomatic. Psychosomatic does not mean 'imaginary'. It means that the body [*soma*] is being affected by the soul [*psyche*].

If repression does not lead to physical illness, it frequently does lead to outbursts when one's 'pressure cooker' becomes too full of repressed emotion. Which of us has not been on the receiving end of someone's disproportionate response to our minor error? We just happened to be their last straw.

Also, emotion is what adds colour to our lives. Restricting the flow of emotion reduces the colour palette of our experience. One way of describing someone who is living a grey, drab life is to say they are depressed. Depression is a broad subject with many different causes and manifestations, but restricted emotion is one of them.

Restricted emotion can have direct effects upon relationships. One of the common difficulties we come across in marriage relationships is the emotional starvation of the wife. When single, most women will have enjoyed the emotionally rich diet of relating to other women. If she marries a man who is emotionally limited, her experience can be akin to moving from a banquet to rations.

We have had clients where one spouse was unwell for a long time. The other spouse was generally supportive but could not be open about the difficulties they experienced in the situation for fear that would have made the other feel guilty or worse in some way. Where they have not known how to process their pain, anger and disappointment etc. they closed those down. That necessarily also closed down the more positive emotions they felt towards their spouse. The ill spouse can recover to find that the other has 'fallen out of love' with them, and now that the ill one has recovered, the other feels free to find love elsewhere. Where we have been able to help the supporting spouse to recognise and deal with their repressed painful emotion, the love has begun to flow again. Sadly, in some cases, for various reasons, that work has not taken place.

Spring opening of a cottage

Imagine that you have a summer cottage on Mt Snowdon, Wales, with water supplied through a pipe from a spring higher up the mountain. You leave the cottage in October, closing it down for the winter. In spring you open up the cottage and one of the first jobs is to switch on the water tap. What do you do when you see brown water flowing out of the tap? Hopefully, you recognise the brown comes from sediment picked up during the winter months as the water stood in the pipe, and so you allow the brown water to flow until eventually the water flows clear.

There can be a similar phenomenon when someone who has closed down emotion begins to express. It is not unusual for the initial flow to be 'brown water', i.e. pain, anger and similar 'bad' emotion. The operating system of someone who has kept a tight rein on emotion would immediately seek to close down these 'bad' ones. Doing so will prevent, or at best delay, the flow of 'good' emotion. It would be a kindness to someone in this position to explain this analogy so that they are not surprised by the 'brown water' and allow it to flow. There may well be practical steps they can take so that the 'brown water' does not cause damage to themselves or others. They will need to be gentle with themselves during this period.

Exercise

1) Go through the sections above and note those points which are most pertinent to the way you live either by commission or omission.

(We will look later at how to work with emotion.)

Chapter Eleven

Cob Walls

We saw that the walls of our house are not separate; we do not have a wall of emotion and a wall of cognition. Rather, emotion and cognition are interwoven in the way that mud, stones and straw are mixed together to construct a cob wall.

Another analogy makes their interplay clearer. Just as fluid flows through a pipe, our cognitions can be likened to pipes through which our emotions (fluid) flow. In my early career I served in Royal Navy warships which had turbines driven by superheated steam. A jet of superheated steam can cut through metal, so strong pipes are needed to carry it. Where an experience is traumatic and involves powerful emotion, the cognitions formed on the basis of that experience will be very strong. When I was two or three, I had an experience which was possibly reasonable within the prevalent culture but would today be considered sexually abusive and at the time was intensely traumatic to me. As a result, I formed some very powerful cognitions about my value and my worth, about others and the treatment I could expect from them.

You will recall my earlier example of going home rather than entering the group late because I believed it was safer to go home than to become the focus of attention. That cognition in my operating system was formed by this early trauma.

Turning from the traumatic to the ordinary, let us imagine a flow of 50,000 gallons of water an hour. Water is not as dangerous as superheated steam and we safely use it every day of our lives, but the volume involved in this case necessitates a large pipe. Similarly, we can have an ordinary experience but if it is repeated frequently the cognition created can be firmly entrenched. When aged twenty-four, I was part of a Christian organisation helping students become disciples of Christ. One discipleship tool was the 'training flat'. An older Christian, me in this case, would have three younger Christians of the same gender living with him for life-on-life discipleship training. The first time we had breakfast together, one of the guys put a jar of jam on the table. I asked him why he'd done that, telling him that you have jam for tea and marmalade at breakfast. I wasn't aware of this cognition until I expressed it, but my early years were during post World War II rationing so this order had been part of my everyday life and had become sufficiently entrenched for me to challenge my friend on his breakfast preferences. (I did not insist he had marmalade!)

One of the guys in this training flat had kindly let me live in a spare room in his flat the year before. After a few weeks I realised that I was tense around him. I didn't know why, so I prayed. My kind friend was a middle-class businessman who was very reserved and quite unemotional. God showed me that his facial expression when not expressing any particular emotion was the same as the one my mother showed when she was about to hit me. As a child I had learnt to watch out when she looked like that if I wanted to avoid being hit, so when as an adult I saw that same expression I became tense. At that time, I was unaware of the knowledge I'm writing about in this book so I didn't know how to deal with it other than to recognise that 'this' was not 'that'.

We can all acknowledge that trauma may well have long-standing and wide-ranging repercussions upon people. It would be a mistake to think that this paradigm is only relevant for people like that. We have had clients whose backgrounds have been good and secure and therefore they have not thought their backgrounds would cause them any problems in their adult lives. As these examples show, our operating systems include beliefs about such mundane matters as marmalade in the morning and jam at teatime, and the interpretation of body language. Where, for instance, one spouse had an operating system designed for an expressive household and the other had an operating system designed for a reserved household, they experienced significant difficulties within their relationship. This was highly frustrating as they both had good backgrounds and loved the Lord and each other, but just couldn't seem to sort out the difficulties. They were greatly helped when they learnt that they had operating systems which were designed to deal with all aspects of life, and their difficulties were largely due to conflicts between their operating systems.

Well done, good and faithful servant!

Exercise

1) Ask the Spirit to help you be aware of any situations where you over-react and note any He mentions.
2) Ask the Spirit to help you be aware of any situations where you insist that things be done in your own way and note any He mentions.
   (You could use these when we look later at how to work with emotion.)

CHAPTER TWELVE

Fourth Heart Area: Spirituality

We saw in the Introduction that there are other spiritual beings apart from God and man, namely angels who were also created by God. The Bible teaches us that some of those angels rebelled against God following their leader who was not satisfied with being the chief angel but aspired to be God. That rebellion was defeated, and it was probably humiliating to its leader that God did not need to stir Himself but was able to defeat the rebellion through loyal angels. That fallen leader seeks revenge but knows he is far too weak to attack God directly, so he directs his hatred to the only place where God is vulnerable. God loves mankind, so the enemy seeks to turn mankind against God and in that way to hurt God.

He was initially successful in causing Adam and Eve to rebel against God. Not only did that separate mankind from God but it brought all mankind under the enemy's dominion, the fruits of which can clearly be seen in the selfishness, pain and suffering rampant throughout the world throughout time.[32]

When God became man incarnate as Jesus Christ, laying aside His majesty and power, He became vulnerable to the enemy who schemed and worked to exploit that vulnerability. To his mind he was successful in that he caused the crucifixion and death of Jesus Christ. Imagine his frustration after the resurrection. He realised that his supposed victory over Jesus was the very means by which Jesus not only opened to all mankind the way of escape from the enemy's rule, but also the way for each who so wished to be adopted into God's family as His son or daughter. That is a privilege way higher than the enemy ever aspired to.

---

[32] I am intrigued that those who are ready to ask, "If God is love and all-powerful, why is there suffering in the world?" never seem to ask, "If man has evolved through the intrinsic selfishness of survival of the fittest, and nature is red in tooth and claw, why is there any good or beauty in the world?"

Well done, good and faithful servant!

As Ephesians 2 reads, we are delivered from the dominion of darkness, transferred to the Kingdom of His beloved son and exalted to sit at God's right hand.

Heavenly pecking order

Pre-salvation	*Post-salvation*
GOD	GOD CHRISTIANS
Angels	Angels
Fallen angels	Fallen angels
Humans	Humans

This table shows God the creator and the spiritual beings He has created in order of authority, the higher exercising authority over the lower. It is very active in that there is an ongoing battle whereby the fallen angels oppress mankind and oppose God and Christians; Christians seek to draw their fellow man to God; God and angels work for Christians and mankind within the self-imposed constraints of their respect for man's free will.

Several aspects of this activity impinge directly upon each one of us and we will now look at those.

Two alternatives, not three

It is clear from the Bible that there are only two sides in this battle. There is God's way or there is the enemy's way. One of the chief pups the enemy sells to mankind is that there are three ways. He insinuates that there is God's way (if He really exists); there is the enemy's way (if you are naive enough to believe in a trident-wielding, tailed, goat-headed being); and there is the individual's way (which is the preferred way, hence Frank Sinatra's *I Did It My Way* becoming an anthem of our age). People are encouraged to think there are some people who are really good, like Mother Theresa, and those live God's ways. There are others who are really evil, like Hitler or Stalin. Depending upon the speaker's worldview, those are either evil personified or are living the enemy's way. However, most of us are doing our own thing in the common land between those extremes and that is fine. The enemy is very happy for people to think like that as he owns the common land! Where successful, this deception results in even a committed Christian living his own way and therefore helping the enemy. Where there are only two ways, if you do not choose God's way then by default you are aiding the enemy.

Topos

You will recall our verse Ephesians 4:26, "Be ye angry and sin not." Verse 27 continues, "...do not give a place to the devil."[33] The Greek word for "place" is *topos*. It is the word used in John 14:3 where Jesus says, "I go to prepare a place for you." So we understand from this that when a person sins, they are giving the enemy a place in the area in which they sinned. The first illustration of this in scripture is in Genesis 4:6-7 where God warns Cain about his anger that "sin is crouching at your door; it desires to have you". In other words, to turn from God's way is to open the door and allow admittance of one who seeks to master you. Imagine a house upon the doorstep of which sits a flea-ridden cat. To sin is to open the door, and as soon as the door is sufficiently ajar, the cat runs into the house.

It is important to understand that a Christian is one who is born again of the Spirit of God and whose body then becomes a temple of the Holy Spirit. As such it is not possible for evil spirits to indwell a Christian, so allowing admittance is not talking about an evil spirit coming into the body of a Christian. Rather, every person has areas of responsibility and authority, and sin invites the enemy into such an area. In other words, it is not that the enemy controls 'us' as in what some call 'demon possession'. Rather, we give the enemy permission to come and influence areas of our life and responsibility. The issue is that many of us fail to take this reality seriously, but the good news is that when we do, we have all the authority we need in Jesus to kick the enemy out.

Once allowed in, the enemy's purpose is to entrench his authority over that area. This is similar to the tactic the Allies employed after D-Day. On D-Day they gained a foothold which they then consolidated into a stronghold from which they extended their control. The enemy's aim is to tempt us away from God's way and thereby allow him a foothold in an area of our life which he will then seek to extend until that area is dominated by him. As Paul says in Romans 6:12, "Do not let sin reign in your mortal bodies so that you obey its evil desires." We see the success of this strategy wherever there is addiction, be that to alcohol, drugs,

---

[33] KJV.

work, success, family or many other examples. Some addictions our society finds unacceptable (such as alcoholism), but some it admires (such as wealth and celebrity).

Trespass

Usually when a Christian becomes aware of sin they will confess, receive forgiveness and so be restored in their relationship with Christ. Reverting to the house illustration used by God with Cain, sin opens the door and confession then closes it again. But one could ask where the cat is and did closing the door have any effect upon the cat? In a real-life situation, the cat would remain inside the house and closing the door would have had no effect upon it whatsoever. This is even more the case in the spiritual realm. Sin was an invitation to the enemy to come into an area of our life and while we continue in that sin, the invitation remains and the enemy is entitled to remain. True confession involves repentance, which is the choice to go God's way and not the enemy's way. It therefore removes the permission for the enemy to remain in that area. In effect he becomes a trespasser. Jesus tells us in John 10:10 that the enemy comes to steal, kill and destroy. Given that agenda, you can be sure he has no qualms about being a trespasser and will continue developing the foothold into a stronghold.

Ejection

One of several reasons why people may suffer from habits that they cannot break, or from what is known as 'besetting sin' is that they have been unaware of these principles of *topos* and trespass. Their view of sin is limited to its effect upon their relationship with Christ and others, and does not recognise the effect in the spiritual realm. Others may be aware of the spiritual realm but think that confession automatically always expels any 'trespasser'. As a result, they sin and confess but do nothing about the trespasser, who uses his influence in that area to encourage them to repeat the sin. When they do, they confess, but again ignore the trespasser. The cycle can continue but with the Christian experiencing increasing hopelessness and despair. The enemy is called the accuser of the brethren. In a situation such as this he will be accusing the Christian that he is weak, hopeless, a disappointment to Christ; that so-called victory is a myth and he might as well stop trying. He will also accuse God to the Christian saying, for example, "If God really loved you, He would help you be victorious. He helps others but not you; He's disappointed in you; He's abandoned you."

A way out of this death spiral is to recognise the spiritual reality and to eject the enemy. He knows that, and so has several ploys to prevent his ejection. One of these is to make it all seem such a special event that only a person with a specific calling or ministry can be effective, certainly not the individual concerned. Another has been to lead people to believe that this is a power encounter. It will involve loud command, shouting and dramatic manifestations until the 'mighty Christian' overcomes. Many Christians, especially British ones with their stiff upper lip, steer clear of such 'drama'. Yet another tactic is to lead well-meaning people to confuse emotional distress with spiritual possession so they spend a long time trying to rebuke an evil spirit out of someone when the person concerned is in fact expressing some of their 'brown water'.

These tactics, especially the last two, have resulted in spiritual warfare being seen as somewhat weird, unusual and to be avoided by the ordinary Christian; whereas, biblically, it is a straightforward and ordinary consequence of seeking to live like Christ and of therefore being in a daily battle between the Kingdom of God and the dominion of darkness. It is straightforward because it is a simple matter of truth and authority.

Truth

There are only two ways: God's and the enemy's.

That statement could invite us to swim in deep waters. Am I saying that people who don't know God can't do anything good? Well, from one perspective no, but from another yes. From our human perspective it is blatantly obvious that there are many people who do much good and are known as good people. That is partly because all of us are created in God's image and so reflect Him to a greater or lesser extent; partly because we all live in a world upheld by and awash with God's general grace which influences us into good. We do need to recognise that this is a human perception of 'good'. We gravitate to a scale where at one end only really evil people like Hitler are 'bad' and at the other are the really good whom we call saints. This scale places most of us in the in-between zone as good. This is not God's perspective. He alone is good. The prophet Isaiah says in Isaiah 64:6, "All of us have become like one who is unclean, and all our righteous acts are like filthy rags." The term "filthy rags" is quite strong. The word "filthy" is a translation of the Hebrew word *iddah*, which literally means 'the bodily fluids from a woman's menstrual cycle'. The word "rags" is a translation of *begged*, meaning 'a rag or garment'. Therefore, these "righteous acts" are considered by God as repugnant as a soiled feminine hygiene product. Isaiah includes himself by saying "all of us". He was a prophet, one of the really good according to our scale, yet he saw himself as part of the filthy rag group. From God's perspective, Isaiah 64:6 could rightly be applied to the whole world. That is a strong statement but is a true description of humanity's problem. We tend to underestimate our predicament but surely the fact that the only solution God could see was for Him to become man and die for us shows that humanity's need is dire.

Having said all that, we are here considering the fourth heart area of spirituality. We all are spiritual beings and live under the dominion of darkness or in the Kingdom of the Jesus. Even when we are reborn into Jesus' Kingdom, we still have free will and so can choose with whom we align ourselves.

Sin is to choose for the enemy and to grant him entitlement. God's way is to align oneself with the truth of God and thereby remove the enemy's entitlement. So when we become aware of sin, the first step is a very simple question: will we change our minds, come into agreement with God and choose His way in that area? If the answer is yes, that transforms the enemy from an invited guest into a trespasser and so he has to submit to a higher authority that commands his departure.

Authority

I very much doubt that you, the reader, would walk into the path of an oncoming twelve-wheeled lorry. It is bigger, heavier and more power-ful than you, and you will most definitely be the one to suffer from the encounter. However, only one thing is needed for you to be able to walk in front of that lorry and cause it to halt. No, you don't become Superman or Superwoman. You wear a police officer's uniform. That invests you with all the authority of the state and, provided you give the driver enough time to see you, the lorry will halt without hesitation. Likewise, in the spiritual realm you do not rely on a power encounter. In power terms, humans (Christian or not) are much weaker than fallen angels. Instead you rely on an authority encounter. The heavenly pecking order shows very clearly that Christians are seated in the heavenly realm at the right hand of God. In addition, Jesus specifically delegated His authority to His disciples: on one occasion to the twelve,[34] on another to the seventy-two,[35] and on a third occassion to every believer.[36] God's desire is that Christians live in the good of all He has done for them on the cross and so become light and salt that transforms the world by extending His Kingdom.

About ten years ago Helen and I were at a conference where the speaker related the experience of someone who had become a Christian after having been a satanist. Apparently, he and other satanists could recognise Christians by their aura and usually they would take the opportunity to mock and tease the Christians they met. From time to time, however, they would see a Christian whose demeanour was such that the satanists knew that Christian was fully aware of, and was walking in, their authority as a child of God. The ex-satanist said they would cross the street to avoid such Christians.

The benefits that flow from a Christian living out of their authority is a whole other subject, though well worth considering. I have given some examples of typical benefits below and if you want to look into this further you could read *One World Two Realms: Operating in Christ's Authority* by Mike Riches. For our purposes, it is sufficient that every Christian realises (1) his or her position as being seated at the right hand of God in the heavenly realm and (2) having Jesus' delegated authority means that when he or she repents of sin, he or she has full authority to rebuke the enemy off that area of their life without let or hindrance. Our practice is to say something like, "In the name and authority of Jesus Christ I command all spirits associated with (whatever the sin is) to leave me now. Go under the feet of Jesus and do not return." We do not know theologically what happens to the spirit, or understand how the spirit realm works beyond what is revealed in scripture, so it seems a good idea to us to send them to Jesus for Him to deal with. Our experience from years of ministry which regularly involves such rebuking is that this is very effective. Many clients have found an increased ability to live effective, victorious and more peaceful lives when they begin to recognise and exercise their authority in the areas they have ceded to the enemy; when they walk as co-heirs with Christ, updating their operating system and living in His authority, free to love and serve.

---

[34] Mark 6:7-13.
[35] Luke 10:17.
[36] Matthew 28:18-20.

Examples

- A young mother disliked the profanity from the workmen repairing her house so bound the spirit of profanity. The swearing stopped.
- A couple were dreading a visit from their in-laws with their constant criticism so prayed that all spirits of complaint and criticism would be silent in their house. The visitors did not complain or criticise.
- A guest in an alpha group continually diverted the discussion by asking 'red herring' questions. A Christian in the group was assigned to keep the spiritual atmosphere clear and the discussion flowed usefully. On the way home, the guest said that he had wanted to ask questions but couldn't.

Common tactics

The enemy is highly intelligent and has many strategies and also lots of experience of manipulating people. *The Screwtape Letters* by C. S. Lewis is a very good primer to help us see how he works. We have seen in our own lives and the lives of our clients three very common tactics he uses against us:

- *Condemnation.* As is her custom, Helen was pouring out her heart in her journal in a time when she was feeling low. God prompted her to look at what she'd written and see how much of it was condemnation or accusation. Helen was surprised to realise that was nearly all of it. God then said very firmly that condemnation never came from Him. All these thoughts were inspired by the enemy. Having been a Christian for many years, Helen was familiar with Romans 8:1 ("There is now no condemnation for those who are in Christ Jesus.") but despite that, these thoughts had come in below the radar, caused her distress and the sense of distancing from God. This was a reminder to keep a vigilant watch upon our self-talk. We need to discern between those thoughts that are from God, from the you God designed, from the you life moulded, and from the enemy, and respond to them appropriately. As the saying goes, you are not responsible for a bird landing on your head but you are for letting it build a nest.

- *Two-ear trick.* The enemy has used this to tip many a Christian into a downward spiral. He whispers temptation into one ear. When the Christian has succumbed, the enemy then whispers condemnation into the other ear. The enemy may then return to the first ear with further temptation, for example along the lines of, "You might as well be killed for a sheep as a lamb." On the Christian again succumbing, back to the second ear with more condemnation, for example, "Now you've really blown it." With sufficient lack of awareness on our part, and we are surprisingly easily made unaware by the enemy manipulating our emotions, he can spiral us downwards out of peace into a darker place. He adapts this trick to our particular character and situation. We can each probably recognise ones he's used against us in the past. Again, the key is to keep a vigilant watch upon our self-talk.

- *Stop or stampede.* The enemy's main tactic is to stop us becoming a Christian and, if that fails, to stop us growing in intimacy with Jesus and into the person God originally designed and our unique destiny. If he cannot stop us, he may try to stampede us; in other words, drive us into ever-increasing busyness. A stark example would be the nineteenth-century preacher Robert Murray McCheyne. After graduating from Edinburgh University at age fourteen in 1827 and leading a Presbyterian congregation of over a thousand at age twenty-three, he worked so hard that his health finally broke. Before dying at age twenty-nine, he wrote, "God gave me a message to deliver and a horse to ride. Alas, I have killed the horse and now I cannot deliver the message." The enemy is aided in this tactic by our society which reflects his dominion in that it tells us that our value depends upon what we do and how successful we are. I would love to have £5 for every time a church leader has complained that when he meets with his peers, the talk will be about the size and success of their congregation; or for every time someone has expressed amazed delight at the realisation that they are a human being not a human doing. The enemy is also aided by our operating system which, unbeknownst to us, impels us in this direction. A recent prayer bulletin included, "I find it nonsensical that Christians 'burn out' when God is the source of strength. Yet in ministry it is endemic, and I am uncomfortably close to it. Please pray for an effective work-life-ministry-spare time balance. Pray for restoration for those who have crossed the line." "Nonsensical ... when God is the source of strength" is such a clear illustration of the gap we saw in 'Mind the gap' between what we believe and how we live. "Yet I am uncomfortably close to it" – a cry of dismay that, knowing what and Who I know, I could be in this place, and perhaps a desperate wish not to be one who crosses the line but with a hint of the inevitability of doing so if God does not break in. Praise the Lord that He often does, but my heart aches that a brother should have been stampeded into this position when he may well have been able to avoid this place by being aware of his operating system and by following the Spirit to update it.

Exercise

1) Where are you in the heavenly pecking order?
2) How, if at all, does this chapter affect your view, and practice, of spiritual warfare?
3) If you suffer under besetting sin, recall how you confess. Do you regain *topos* or cede it?
4) Think of your areas of responsibility (home, family, church, work etc.). To what extent do you safeguard the spiritual atmosphere? Do you allow the enemy free reign[37] by default?
5) Ask the Holy Spirit if there are improvements He would like you to use your authority to make in any area.
6) Do you recognise any of the enemy's tactics in your life? How could you more effectively defeat them?

---

[37] Pun intended!

CHAPTER THIRTEEN

The Dichotomy Within Us

We are now at the sixth of the seven aspects of our paradigm (see end of chapter 3 for a reminder of the seven).

A game

Let us play a little game. Take a sheet of paper and place it in landscape so that the long sides are at the top and bottom. Then in roughly the middle place a dot to mark the date you were born...

○
born

...and then draw a line from the dot to the righthand margin.

○———————————————————————
born

Then place another dot on that line to mark the date at which, if you had a conversion experience, you became a Christian, or by which, if you did not have a conversion experience, you were sure you were a Christian.

born   reborn

Now, some Christians were reborn in a context where they learnt about living in the power of the Spirit and were filled by Him at the same time that they became Christians, but for others, like myself, this was experienced subsequent to rebirth. In either case place another dot under the line to mark that point.

Well done, good and faithful servant!

born   reborn   Spirit-filled

Now return to the birth point and place a dot to left at the time that you were conceived.

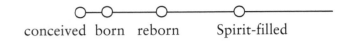

conceived born reborn   Spirit-filled

Many of you will have quite accurately placed that nine months before birth but others may have spotted the 'trick' (or remembered from the Introduction) and marked a dot on the far left hand margin. Ephesians 1:4 tells us that God chose us in Christ before the foundation of the world which means that God conceived us before then too.

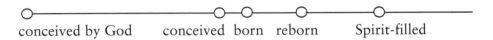

conceived by God   conceived born reborn   Spirit-filled

Our understanding from Psalm 139 and similar scriptures is not that God conceived of humanity in general but rather that He conceived each one of us as specific individuals to be born at a specific place in a specific time. This understanding is known to some as Original Design, to others as Spiritual DNA, to others as their Kingdom Blueprint. Whatever the phrase, it means that God planned you before the universe and waited expectantly for long ages for you to be born. As parents we know the excitement when our child is born after nine months; how much more was God's excitement with such a long period between your conception and birth! However, whilst God was thrilled at your birth, it was even more thrilling at your rebirth when you came into His family and began to relate to Him. When you learnt about living in the Spirit, you had the power to live out His Original Design for you and move into the Unique Destiny Ephesians 2:10 shows He has prepared.

This line represents the You God Designed.

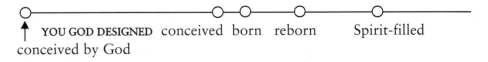

↑ **YOU GOD DESIGNED** conceived born reborn   Spirit-filled
conceived by God

100

The You God Designed

This You God Designed is a wonderful truth. It can be extraordinarily helpful, especially to decisions about how you spend your life.

James 1 teaches that if we lack wisdom, we can ask God and He will give it to us. When parents ask Him to reveal something of their child's Original Design, it not only helps them parent but also, when shared, communicates to the child their true value and worth. That is wonderfully reassuring during puberty with its cry of, "Who am I?"

Knowing the Original Design of your fellow Christians and teammates is a great aid to effective unity.

Praying Original Design can also be an effective evangelistic tool. Our experience in helping to found a church for non-churched youth includes a practice of asking youth for permission to pray for them by asking God to reveal something of how He made them. We would write down what we heard so the person could take it away. Also, when two or three of us prayed and wrote, and the revelation we each heard was similar (as was often the case), the person prayed for could see that we had not copied each other, which they could have thought if we hadn't written but had just spoken in turn. This is a very effective way of demonstrating that God is real and knows and loves them. Having prayed for hundreds of people in this way, we have seen some become Christians and know of one who did not continue with a planned suicide because he saw the card on which his Original Design was written and that gave him hope.

The dichotomy

You may be asking, "Where is the dichotomy which this section is supposed to be about?"

If you return to your timeline, please draw a vertical line of any length you choose from a point between your physical conception and birth. Mark that with an A.

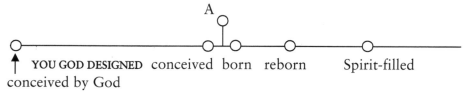

↑ YOU GOD DESIGNED   conceived   born   reborn   Spirit-filled
conceived by God

That is the point from which you began to experience life. Please continue that line towards the right-hand margin parallel to the lower

Well done, good and faithful servant!

timeline. Then draw a line upwards vertically from the point of your beginning rebirth to your life experience line and mark that with a B. Then continue the line A-B towards the right-hand margin.

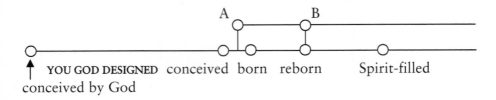

Throughout that period A-B your experiences led to the creation and entrenchment of your operating system. That line and its continuance represents the You Life Moulded.

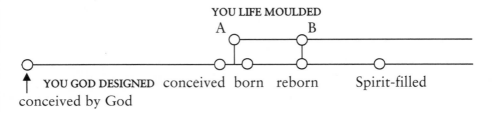

The dichotomy lies between the two Yous: the You God Designed and the You Life Moulded.

A coaxial cable such as a television aerial illustrates the two Yous. The central wire represents the You God Designed.

Around that wired there is a hard plastic insulation which represents the way that as life wounds us we learn to harden our emotions.

There is then a copper braid which represents the cognitions experience teaches us.

The plastic sleeve then represents our body.

The insulation and braiding represent the You Life Moulded.

The You Life Moulded

You will notice that the You Life Moulded runs around and follows the You God Designed. This reflects two truths.

- There will be aspects of the You Life Moulded that run along the same lines as the You God Designed. So, part of my Original Design is that I am a pioneer. Hence it is not surprising that aged sixty, when others are planning to retire, I set out on a new venture of helping to establish a church for non-churched youth which in itself was a pioneering venture ten years ago. That same pioneering tendency meant that as a child I would often rebel and venture into forbidden territory e.g. aged seven climbing freestyle on bungalow roofs which were only bare timber.

- There are aspects of the You Life Moulded which are intrinsic to how you have learnt to live but which are not part of the essential You. The You Life Moulded is the one with which we are most familiar, but is not the one who is truly you.

Looking again at the coaxial cable, we know that it is not until the aerial is connected to a power source that it becomes live. Similarly, it is not until we are reborn that our spirit becomes alive, we become wholly alive. Changing the physics slightly, light is emitted as a current flows through a wire and it is as the power of the Holy Spirit flows through the You God Designed that the light of Christ can transform the You Life Moulded so that, in the words of 2 Corinthians 3:18, we reflect His glory.

Our society encourages us to look within to find the real you. One example would be Mariah Carey singing that there's a hero if you look inside your heart.

According to Wikipedia:[38]

> Carey has described how the song was never her favourite, however, after all the fan letters and messages she received about the song, she felt the need to perform it as often as possible. In an interview with Fred Bronson Carey described the song's meaning to her and to fans:

> "One person could say that 'hero' is a schmaltzy piece of garbage, but another person can write to me a letter and say, 'I've considered committing suicide every day of my life for the last ten years until I heard that song and I realized after all I can be my own hero.' And that, that's an unexplainable feeling, like I've done something with my life, y'know?... It meant something to someone."

Clearly it can be really helpful to look within. When you do, you will find the You Life Moulded.

---

[38] *https://en.wikipedia.org/wiki/Hero_(Mariah_Carey_song)#cite_note-nickson8-11*

As we have seen, the You Life Moulded is built up over the inner core of the You God Designed. That means there are many areas which have much good in them. Also, whilst the You Life Moulded is built up through our responses to our natal environment, in many cases parents and carers are genuinely seeking to love in the best way they can so that environment can contain much that is wise, good and healthy. We must not forget that, despite all the pain and suffering flowing from the dominion of darkness and our inherent selfishness, this world still exhibits much of the goodness, wisdom and love of God. We must not fall into the trap of thinking that the You Life Moulded is all bad. No, there is much good in it, so the level of self-awareness reflected in the song *Hero* can be transformative.

Yet it is not the abundant life that Jesus promises. There can be so much more. Christ dying on the cross paid the penalty for mankind's sin so anyone can come to God for forgiveness and rebirth into His family. That can be called the legal aspect of redemption, justification. When rebirth is lived out there will be changes in speech and behaviour. Those can be called becoming more like the Jesus we follow, sanctification. We often experience difficulties with sanctification and some of those can be the fruit of those aspects of our natal operating system, the You Life Moulded, that do not reflect the goodness, wisdom and love of God. Being transformed by the Spirit helping us update that operating system is another aspect of redemption. It is taking the gospel to the unevangelised parts of the soul. This enables us increasingly to become the unique You God Designed, to live out our unique Destiny in the abundant life made possible by Jesus' death and resurrection.

Galatians 5:17

In this verse Paul says, "The sinful nature desires what is contrary to the Spirit, and the Spirit what is contrary to the sinful nature. They are in conflict with each other, so that you do not do what you want."

Paul knew this conflict well as a serious part of his daily experience. In 1 Corinthians 9:27 he says, "No, I beat my body and make it my slave so that after I have preached to others, I myself will not be disqualified for the prize." My own experience, and I imagine that of many others too, is that we can live for large parts of our time as if there is no such conflict.

Some, like me, are of an older generation. Our operating system was moulded when the United Kingdom had a purportedly Christian society so our You Life Moulded can be respectable and 'Christian'. This can lull us into a powerless peace whereas in 1 Corinthians 4:20 Paul says the Kingdom of God is not a matter of talk but of power.

For others who were raised in the postmodern era where there is no meta-narrative, tolerance is the key value. Indeed, the only thing that cannot be tolerated is the suggestion that there is 'right or wrong'. For such, 'battle' can be almost too countercultural a concept.

Even where we recognise this well-known conflict, familiarity with the verse easily leads us to limit the application of Galatians 5:17. When we think of the "sinful nature" or, as in other versions, the "flesh", we most easily think of behaviours such as pride, envy, wrath, gluttony, lust, sloth and greed – the seven deadly sins – and we tend to think of those as the battle areas. The battle areas are in fact far more wide-ranging. As we saw above, our operating system covers every aspect of life such as marmalade for breakfast, jam for tea, and interpretation of body language. The war is in fact whether we will live by our natal operating system as the You Life Moulded or whether we will cooperate with the Spirit in updating that operating system where He thinks necessary and live as the You God Designed.

Some might think it is a little radical to think that such mundane aspects of life are part of a spiritual battle. That suggestion only makes sense if you buy into the thesis discussed previously that there are three alternatives, not two. When you recognise that there are only two alternatives, it is clear that every aspect of life is effectively a spiritual choice.

We see this reality, that there are only two alternatives, reflected in John 15:5 where Jesus taught, "Apart from me you can do nothing." It is obvious from the fact that many people who do not acknowledge Jesus are very productive, that He did not mean this literally. Hebrews 11:6 which says that "without faith it is impossible to please him" would suggest that in John 15:5 Jesus could rightly be understood to be saying that "without faith in me it is impossible to do anything to please God". Romans 14:23, which is talking about eating and drinking, makes this even more starkly clear by saying, "Everything that does not come from faith is sin."

If we consider our two Yous in the light of these scriptures, we see we each have an operating system that functions automatically but in so doing will by definition be "apart from me [Jesus]", "without faith" and therefore "is sin", as anything that is not God's way is the enemy's way. Our operating system necessarily opens us up to spiritual oppression. No wonder Paul cries out in Romans 7:24, "What a wretched man I am! Who will rescue me from this body of death?"

We are possibly in most peril when we do not echo Paul's cry – those times when we excuse ourselves by saying, "It's just the way I'm made," "I just don't do emotion," "That's the way we do it." Yet it is when we hear ourselves say or think these excuses that we can recognise the enemy within. Emilio Mola, a nationalist general during the Spanish Civil War, told a journalist in 1936 that as his four columns of troops approached Madrid, a fifth column of supporters inside the city would undermine the Government from within. The You Life Moulded was formed while you were a child living under the dominion of darkness. Being more comfortable within that dominion, the You Life Moulded is an indwelling fifth column, always choosing to undermine your growth into the You God Designed.

At times we do echo Paul's cry, and we can experience growth, but where we are not aware of the fundamental effect of our operating system upon the way we live, we can be frustrated that we do not grow in godliness as much as we would like. The chief value in understanding this paradigm is that it liberates us actively to cooperate with the Spirit in updating our operating system. We can align ourselves with God's chief desire that we be transformed in character to become like Jesus.

One thing is certain. One of your two Yous will be overruled. Either you will follow your operating system which will please the You Life Moulded but overrule the You God Designed; or you will follow the Holy Spirit in updating your operating system and living as the You God Designed. In that case, the You Life Moulded will be overruled.

The more significant question is, "Who else do you choose to please?" Living as the You Life Moulded pleases the enemy and grieves God, whilst living as the You God Designed frustrates the enemy and delights Jesus because He sees in you the fruit of the travail of His soul. This is what I believe is termed a 'no-brainer'! Engage in the battle; please God, and choose to live as the You God Designed and to update the You Life Moulded.

Purposes and schemes

Have you ever given a seminar, lesson or sermon; led a meeting at church or work? You prayed, prepared and did it as well as you could but then you wish you knew how well it had gone. You'd like to ask people but don't want to because that may seem like fishing for compliments. Anyway, you'd think they were only saying what they thought you wanted to hear. So you don't ask and shrug off your insecurity with differing amounts of success. Or is that only me?

It can be even worse at work where colleagues and bosses are quick to point out mistakes but usually do not mention a job well done.

Some of us are supremely confident and don't identify with this at all but I suspect most, to a greater or lesser extent, suffer some such dis-ease. The enemy loves to play on that and has a lot of opportunity because, whatever criterion you use to measure how 'it' went, there will always be another by which 'it' went worse. Was it an evangelistic talk and two people became Christians? There was a full room so why not more saved? You rambled and lost their attention; you didn't make a clear enough altar call; you made people feel under the spotlight – so more didn't respond.

> *For we are God's workmanship, created in Christ Jesus to do good works, which God prepared in advance for us to do.*
>
> *Ephesians 2:10*

As you walk in the Spirit, He leads you into works God prepared for you in advance.

> *It is God who works in you to will and to act according to his good purpose.*
>
> *Philippians 2:13*

So God has a purpose for each work that He leads you into.

It is clear from a general reading of scripture that His desire is to be able to commend you, "Well done, good and faithful servant."

So the only criterion which you have to satisfy *in anything* is whether or not you were faithful. The most straightforward way of knowing that is to ask Him, beforehand, what His purpose for you is in the conversation, meeting, whatever good work you are about to embark upon. Then afterwards you ask Him if you were faithful. If He shows you any way in which you weren't, you apologise; that removes any ground for accusation so you move on in peace to implement the new learning. If you were faithful, you were; that extinguishes any accusation the enemy might wish to throw at you.

We recognise that the enemy always seeks to thwart God's purpose so we also pray beforehand asking God to let us know the enemy's schemes in the situation. When He tells us, we examine ourselves to see if there is anything in us that buys into those schemes. If there is, we '5R' that (as explained in chapter 15) and clothe ourselves in the replacement blessing. Forewarned is forearmed, so during the 'work' we will be on the lookout and exercising our authority to close those schemes down.

It is now our practice at the start of every day, before any meeting, on the way to any event, to pray purposes and schemes. Doing so has greatly contributed to the increased peace and power we have experienced in the last decade.

Exercise

1) Ask God for your Original Design. One way would be for you and your friends/family/house group together to each write their name on an A4 sheet of paper. Place the sheets in the middle and then each take a sheet, ask God to reveal one, two or three aspects of His Original Design for the person named, fold the sheet over to hide what you wrote and put it back in the middle. When everyone has taken each sheet and prayed, each person will have some aspects of their Original Design.

2) To what extent do you recognise in your daily life the dichotomy between the two Yous? Ask the Spirit if there are changes He would like you to make.

3) Are there areas where the Spirit would like you to engage more proactively in the Galatians 5 battle?

4) Part of Ignatian spirituality is the daily *Examen* where you review your day to thank God for the blessings and see one 'failure' you could improve. You could adapt this to ask the Spirit to show you if there was one way you grieved Him and ask His help instead to live as the You God Designed in that place.

5) Pray purposes and schemes as suggested and thank God for the blessings that flow.

CHAPTER FOURTEEN

Q: How? A: Play Detective

How do we live as the You God Designed and update the You Life Moulded?

The first step is to echo Paul in Romans 7:25 – "Thanks be to God-through Jesus Christ our Lord!" – and recognise the source of our help. Not only has His cross worked our salvation from condemnation but His resurrection has imputed to us His righteousness. No longer worthy of punishment, because Jesus died in our place God considers us to be as innocent as Jesus. But Jesus died to make something even greater than that possible. As He said in John 16:7, "Unless I go away, the Counsellor will not come to you; but if I go, I will send Him to you." And verse 13: "When He, the Spirit of truth, comes, He will guide you into all truth." "All truth" undoubtedly includes the revelation and recollection which enabled the Gospels to be written but should not be restricted to that. It includes us "being transformed into [Jesus'] likeness with ever increasing glory, which comes from the Lord who is the Spirit"[39] that we will "become mature, attaining to the whole measure of the fullness of Christ"[40]; and "speaking the truth in love, we will in all things grow up into ... Christ"[41].

Our biggest problem with the You Life Moulded is that our operating system functions automatically in our subconscious, which means we are usually not aware of it. Part of the truth into which the Holy Spirit wishes to lead us individually is into awareness of our operating system. One way of expressing this is that we are taking the gospel to the unevangelised parts of our soul. We follow the Holy Spirit by being sensitive to His leading and that means in very practical ways we play detective.

---

[39] 2 Corinthians 3:18.
[40] Ephesians 4:13.
[41] Ephesians 4:15.

How does the Holy Spirit lead us?

Our birthright of hearing God is vital to our following the Holy Spirit as He leads us into the truth that will update our operating system. We do not have to rely upon vague impressions but we can ask Him specific questions and receive His specific answers as we follow His clues.

[1] We play detective *to discover if there are any family traits by asking Him to reveal any relevant ones.* It may be that as we think with Him about our family line, we can see traits relevant to the issue He has brought to our attention. Sometimes He may reveal aspects of our family line that happened before the time of which we have knowledge.

[2] We play detective *to uncover non-godly cognitions by catching what we hear and think:*

- black-and-white language like 'always', and 'never';
- rules such as 'must', 'should' – what we call an attack of the should-ers.

These are clues to be followed up. We follow the clues by 'drop-down'. That is, we ask ourselves, "Because?" or, "What does that mean to me?" The Holy Spirit helps us become aware of the answer to that. We then follow that answer with another drop-down and repeat the process until we sense from Him that we have gone as far down into our operating system as He wants us to at this time. We will now have some awareness of the cognition and be able to pray into it.

In chapter 16 I explain how the Spirit leads us in updating particular areas of our operating system but here I include an extract to demonstrate how the drop-down works. The questions I asked are in italic font. I then waited on the Spirit to show me what my operating system answer of the next step was. Those awarenesses the Spirit gave are underlined.

When following where He led me, it is useful to bear in mind our three sets of cognitions described in chapter 9 and that influential non-godly beliefs are often formed before we developed reason so the answers might not make rational sense. In this case, the answer "Mum" is a jump that might surprise some readers.

Possibly prompted by the Spirit, the question came to mind, "<u>Why the urgency?</u>"

The urgency is because [pause to become aware] <u>these have to be done</u> … *because* [pause to become aware] <u>I have to have everything tidy</u> …

because [pause to become aware] <u>Mum likes it that way</u> ... *and that means* [pause to become aware] <u>if it's not, she's upset</u> .... *and that means* [pause to become aware] <u>she hits me or is in a mood, either way I've got it wrong again, caused trouble</u> ... *because* [pause to become aware] <u>I always cause trouble. I can never be good enough no matter how hard I try</u> ... *and that means* [pause to become aware] <u>she's dangerous and will get me</u> ... *so* [pause to become aware] <u>keep on trying – but it's hopeless. I'll never be good enough</u> ... *and that means*[42] [pause to become aware] <u>but at least I can stop her attacking me.</u>"

The script clearly shows the non-godly beliefs the Spirit showed me that I formed as a little lad wholly dependent upon my mum:

1) "I have to have everything tidy."
2) "She's dangerous and will get me."
3) "I always cause trouble."
4) "I can never be good enough."
5) "It's hopeless."
6) "I have to keep on trying."
7) "Keeping Mum happy keeps me safe."

They reflect the powerlessness of a child and the consequence that pleasing the carer is all-important. Depending how young the child was when the cognition was formed, it can literally be a matter of life and death.

[3] We play detective *to uncover the emotional component of our operating system by paying attention to our feelings,* remembering that emotion is to the soul as pain is to the body. Clearly pleasant feelings can be enjoyed as, for example, one would enjoy bathing hot feet in cool water. It is the jarring or unpleasant feelings that we need to heed. These can be fleeting or they may be strong.

Do we have to deal with the emotions immediately? Perhaps, but we would suggest you follow the principles:

---

[42] "I can stop her attacking me" is not really a 'that means' response but it is what came to me. This illustrates that the Holy Spirit can use 'that means' to help you become aware of (1) a deeper level of your operating system, or (2) conclusions, vows, judgements or the like which you have formed, as He did for me here.

- Not necessarily *now* – following feelings is not an excuse to emote inappropriately ("I feel it and so must express it *now.*") We all have experience of the damage caused by intemperate speech and action.
- Nor *no time* – not wishing someone to be on the receiving end of our emotion, or not wishing to make a mountain out of a molehill, can lead to 'no time'. In other words, we just ignore the emotion and add it to our store of repression.

As an aside, we have experienced from several different churches over the years that a time can come when people feel sufficiently close to one another to act as if sarcasm and mocking humour are signs of intimacy. When you are on the receiving end, it can be difficult to let people know you don't like this humour because you feel you may be seen to be making a mountain out of a molehill because it was 'only a joke'. One of our sons-in-law found a very good solution. We are all familiar with flushing the toilet to get rid of waste. His practice was that if someone said something that was sarcastic or mocking, he would reply with a humorous, "I'll flush that." This reminded him not to buy into the untruth and also, in a light manner, let the speaker know that what was said was inappropriate. At a time in our church where people were suffering lots of 'cuts' from this sort of humour, "I'll flush that" was key to our church becoming much more honouring of one another.

To return to the main flow, the better approach than 'now' or 'no time' can be:

- Make *another time.* You may be in conversation with someone and feel a twinge of hurt at something they say. If that is not an appropriate time to deal with the emotion, you could 'file it' and make a mental note with the Holy Spirit that you will talk to Him about it at a specific later time. At that 'made time' ask Him to help you be back in the situation and to become aware of what was disturbing you.

He may bring to mind the wound, memory or event about which He wishes you to become aware so that He can heal this aspect of your operating system. Follow where He leads, be there and express to Him all you feel in that place. This is pouring out your heart to God as exemplified by David. Psalm 140 is a good example. In verse 10 he says, "Let burning coals fall down on their heads, or throw them into the fire, or into deep pits from which they can't escape."[43] This scripture is not intended to teach us appropriate behaviour towards those who hurt us. It is intended to teach us to be brutally frank in telling God exactly how we feel. We do that, not because God doesn't know but because we don't. One of the safety systems God has created within each of us is that painful events are lodged in our subconscious so we are largely unaware of them. By expressing verbally, we become aware.

When we feel we have expressed everything at this time we would:

- ask Jesus where He is in the situation – being omnipresent He was there but we were probably not aware of Him, especially where the experience predates our rebirth;
- ask Him to show us His perspective on the experience;
- give the feelings we expressed to Him (so it can be useful to have expressed them on paper) and see how He responds. In all the many times we have done this personally or with clients, we have not seen Him respond in the same way. He knows exactly what the experience meant to the person and what response will most help them.

It can then be good to return to the place to which He took you and see how it feels now. Many times it is transformed in that the pain is not there. Sometimes it is not wholly dealt with. In such a case ask the Holy Spirit if there is something more to deal with at that time or to be left until a later time. It has been around for a long time so there is no urgency in clearing it all in one go.

In the course of expressing your feelings, you may have become aware of some non-godly cognitions, someone to forgive, vows, curses, unhealthy soul ties. It is good to pray those through too. This is what we call housekeeping. We talk about how to pray into these in the next chapter.

Someone may be concerned either that they are going to have to go back through every life experience in this way, or that they will be re-traumatised by returning to the originating experience. This is not the case because of who God is and because of the nature of the operating system.

Firstly, God loves you deeply and will always honour you and will never shame you. Now, some of these wounds are deep and have not

---

[43] NLT.

been healed. If you were to have a deep cut on your thigh and it healed without being cleaned first, it may become tender. You will not want it to be touched and will be sensitive about how you use it or let it be touched. Similarly, with emotional wounds that have not been healed we can be 'touchy'. We probably all have known someone to whom you never talk about certain matters because you know they would react badly. That reaction is an indication of possible unhealed emotional pain.

Where there is a deep physical wound, a nurse would clean out the deep wound thoroughly. That can be unpleasant but she will be careful not to hurt you too much. Indeed, some cleansing can take place under anaesthetic if it would be too painful without. Likewise, there may well be pain in revisiting the wound, but God will never lead us into more than He knows He can enable us to bear. That is why in my case He took several years thoroughly to heal my early experience.

Secondly, the operating system is built up by beliefs that worked for you in your family situation. If they had not worked, they would not have been adopted. They did work and so you continued to use them and they became entrenched. The components are akin to the writing in a stick of seaside rock. No matter where along the stick you cut, you will find the same pattern. So, if God wants to update your operating system, He does not have to take you back to the originating experience but can cut into your life at any point to access the pattern He wants to update. This brings two encouragements.

- You do not have to deal with every experience because the updating at one point may effectively update other similar points also.
- Nor does He have to take you back to the traumatising event. Indeed, we have seen in our own and clients' experiences that where there has been trauma the Lord will often help the client to access the operating system at a non-traumatic event. As they learn to 'live by that update' and become stronger emotionally, He can lead nearer to the trauma until it can be accessed without re-traumatisation if He deems such access necessary.

By following these clues with the Holy Spirit, you will have become aware of aspects of your operating system, the You Life Moulded, that He wishes you to update. You implement the update by repentance.

CHAPTER FIFTEEN

Repentance

This seventh aspect of our Paradigm is fundamental to our Christian life. When people heard they had crucified the Messiah and, "convicted deeply", asked Peter, "What should we do?"[44] his reply[45] was that they should repent and be baptised. Our Christian life continues in the same way; as Paul says in Colossians 2:6, "...so then, just as you received Christ Jesus as Lord, continue to live in him." We do not need to repeat our baptism but we do need to repent whenever we sin. Over the years we have been shown many different prayers of repentance and they are all very similar (as you would expect given the Bible's clarity). Our prayer aide (see Appendix) reflects these with three emphases that can easily be overlooked in practice: namely relational, rebuke and replace.

Before we look at this prayer aide it is absolutely vital to say that the purpose of this aide is not that it becomes a formula, liturgical or rote but that it enables the one praying to grasp the essential principles and then pray accordingly. The language should be changed to whatever the pray-er finds meaningful but the principles need to be observed. You don't have to pray every part exactly in this order but the principles do build upon one another.

5R-ing

As an *aide memoir,* each of the five principles begins with an 'R' and by way of shorthand we refer to this prayer as 5R-ing. Let us look at each R in turn.

---

[44] Acts 2:37.
[45] Verse 38.

RECOGNISE

Imagine that you are walking through life and the Holy Spirit draws to your attention something that is not godly. It is therefore sin and He is inviting you to recognise it as such, so the first principle is to agree with Him and recognise that this is sin.

How does the Holy Spirit draw to your attention something that is not godly?

Familiar ways will be conviction (i.e. that sense He gives); conscience; becoming aware through scripture; or someone's admonition or reaction. Possibly new ones would be becoming aware of what you say, think and feel and following those clues.

REPENT

On your imaginary journey you will doubtless have stopped because you do not want to continue in that sin. You would prefer to walk in godliness so the second principle is to repent: a clear choice of the will that from this point you turn your back on that sin, renounce it and declare that you will walk God's way.

RELEASE AND RECEIVE FORGIVENESS

Sin is not some neutral abstract. It is a personal affront to God for which we need to apologise and be forgiven. It is also unlikely only to have offended God but may also have damaged others and ourselves, so apology and forgiveness are needed there too. As Jesus taught in the Lord's prayer, our sins are forgiven as we forgive others. An *aide memoire* for forgiveness is to think of a Celtic cross. The horizontal bar reminds us to release forgiveness to others, the circle or O reminds us to forgive ourselves, and the vertical reminds us to ask for and receive forgiveness from God.

You will see from our prayer aide that after forgiving others in general terms we suggest you pause to ask God if there is anyone you specifically need to mention. He knows you may overlook, or not be aware of, someone, and this is an important aspect that helps your prayer be relational and not become formulaic.

You will also see that after asking God for forgiveness we suggest that you pause to become aware of His actually forgiving you. Once you have been a Christian for a while, and have become familiar with the unlimited and free forgiveness Jesus won for us at the cross, His experience of our confessing can be similar to yours if I were to slap you across the cheek, then apologise and thank you for forgiving me, and walk out of the room. You would be left with a stinging cheek and wishing that you had been involved in that transaction between us. We don't want to leave Jesus feeling He wished He had been given the chance to respond to our confession. What's more, we find that at times Jesus responds in a very significant way when given the opportunity granted by our pausing to receive His forgiveness.

REBUKE

When we don't take seriously Paul's injunction in Ephesians 6 to be alert because of the incessant spiritual battle in which we are engaged, we can reduce sin and repentance to our relationships with God and others, overlooking the enemy dimension. All sin is to side with the enemy and to invite Him into that area. It is therefore important that we do not omit rebuke from our prayer. We are aware of a situation where a person struggled unsuccessfully with impurity, which they intensely disliked but they repeatedly failed to walk in the purity they longed for. A significant step to their freedom was recognising that the enemy had never been rebuked off that area so a stronghold had been established. This was destroyed when rebuking became part of the prayer of repentance.

REPLACE

We know from Jesus' story of the house that was cleaned out but reoccupied when it was left empty, Matthew 12:45, that it is important whenever we regain ground from the enemy that that area be filled with the Holy Spirit. That is where replacement begins.

If you think about the image of your journey so far, you recognised you were *walking a way you'd chosen* and not God's way, so you *stood still*. You then repented, which means you turned 180° with your back to your way, intending to walk in God's way. You've been forgiven, broken off any hold the enemy had and now want to know what God's way for you is. A common error is to decide yourself what that way is. Perhaps you know a scriptural alternative to the sin so you think that is the way God would want you to follow. Can you see that if you now walk in that way, it may again be *walking a way you've chosen?* In effect you may well have turned another 180° onto a way that is different to the sin but is still your own way.

We suggest that rather than executing this 360° you *ask the Holy Spirit to show you what God's way is for you.* Returning to the example of impurity, they knew from scripture that Jesus wants us to be pure so they had thought repentance meant they needed to walk in purity. Their discouragement was that they couldn't. We suggested they ask God for His replacement. They heard a clear affirmation of God's love. That was highly meaningful because as a child they lived in an environment where they had not received comfort when hurt. So their operating system included the cognition that they had to comfort themselves. When older, they found impurity was very comforting. Regardless of how much they tried to walk in purity, whenever life hurt them, their operating system automatically led them into the impure comfort. After they had experienced this clear affirmation of God's love, they knew they could now turn to God for comfort. From that point, when hurt they began to return again to God's love and receive His comfort. As they walked in God's replacement, they experienced a level of purity which previously would have seemed an impossible fantasy.

The rationale behind asking God for the replacement rather than following your own, even if you choose a scriptural one, is that you probably do not know how your operating system is working. So ask the God who does! He is omnipresent and so has been with you every moment of your life. He knows you intimately, including exactly how your operating system works and needs updating.

Additional comments

You will see that the aide on page 134 is entitled 'Holistic [5R] Prayer' and that the five Rs are set out under 'Historical and Cognitive' and 'Emotional' subheadings with no separate prayer for the 'Spiritual'. Spiritual oppression is always a consequence of the enemy being given permission through one of the other three aspects of our operating system. Once that permission has been removed, the trespasser can be evicted, so the Spiritual is incorporated into the other three.

There are one or two things to say about those other three aspects of the aide.

Well done, good and faithful servant!

- The aide says 'forebears'. Some people prefer 'ancestors', others prefer a phrase such as 'my family line before me'. It is your prayer so say whatever covers the situation and is meaningful to you.
- The blank for the sin can be easily understood for something like abandonment where a parent has divorced and so brought abandonment into the family line but what about where a parent dies prematurely by accident or illness? They did not sin but they will have abandoned their child. That child will have had various reactions to being abandoned. Where those were sinful, if not brought to the cross those sinful reactions would pass down the line. It is quite a mouthful to say something like 'the sinful reactions of one of my forbears to having been abandoned by their forbear'. So we prefer to keep to the simple wording 'sins of abandonment' but explain this broader meaning.
- There are other historical sins to which this principle would apply.

COGNITIVE

- A key to a good godly belief is to be clear about the non-godly belief, so that may need a little clarifying with the Holy Spirit so that 'it rings true' to how your operating system actually works in life.
- It is important to remember that (1) the non-godly belief is like a well-worn rut that you drive along automatically; (2) unless God works miraculously, it takes about six weeks for the godly belief you receive to become well entrenched as the replacement update in your operating system; (3) you are in a battle where the enemy will work against that update becoming effective. We therefore suggest that in the 'Replacement' section you pause in the prayer after you have received the revelation from the Holy Spirit to condense it into an easily useable form. You do not want James Bond's AR-7 sniper rifle[46] that needs to be unpacked and put together before it can be fired. You need a sword that can be wielded swiftly. Some clients hear in words and receive a

---

[46] As in *From Russia With Love.*

paragraph. Others hear by picture and receive a movie. In either case a 'mini workshop' would be useful to arrive at the verbal or pictorial sword.

- Where a non-godly cognition is about your identity, we would refer to it as a False Identity Statement. You will recognise these because they follow the phrase "I am"; for example, "I'm stupid", "I'm ugly", "I'm worthless" were some of mine. God will replace these with a True Identity Statement which again will complete the phrase beginning "I am". We recommend it is inadequate for a replacement simply to be a negative – for example, "I am not stupid" – because the emphatic word in that phrase is "stupid" so it actually reinforces the False Identity Statement. As a general principle, it is better for replacement truth to be expressed in a positive form.

EMOTIONAL

- When explaining above how to play detective in the emotional, we have given the process where there is a deep or strong emotion involved. There will be times where it won't be appropriate to go that deep, but you will simply want to 'make time' to express your emotions appropriately with the Lord and to become aware of His presence and His perspective on the situation involved.

REBUKING

- We can become aware of a judgement (for example, "She's lazy."); a vow ("I'll never let anyone hurt me like that again."); a curse, which is a word spoken by someone in authority over you, and you receive that word (for example, "You'll never make anything of yourself.") In these cases, when rebuking, our practice would be to add a phrase such as, "In Jesus' Name and Authority, I take the sword of the Spirit and break the curse/vow/judgement and command all spirits empowering and associated with this curse/vow/judgement..." and then continue the ejection.

UNHEALTHY SOUL TIES

- These can be formed either:
  - by sexual intercourse, as it is part of the creation order that in consummation a man and woman become one;[47] or
  - by a pattern of relating where one party is unable to be wholly themselves free from the other (who often may have some authority over the other by family tie, by organisational role or by the nature of their relationship).
- If we were praying for John to be released from an unhealthy soul tie with Jane, when rebuking, our practice would be to add a phrase such as, "In Jesus' Name and Authority, I take the sword of the Spirit and break John's unhealthy soul ties with Jane and release John to be wholly himself, free from Jane, and release Jane to be wholly herself, free from John, and command all spirits empowering and associated with this unhealthy soul tie etc."

REPLACEMENT

- Prayer brings about significant transactions in the spiritual realm. For many who, like me, had a conversion experience, a few words that took about a minute to pray brought about a radical deliverance from the dominion of darkness and transfer into the Kingdom of light. Similarly, even when padded out, a wedding service lasts about half an hour and the actual marriage part of the service takes about five minutes but from that point they are no longer two but one in God's eyes.
- For the significance of the conversion or marriage to be realised, the prayer needs to be lived out on a daily basis.
- The same is true for these prayers of repentance. The prayer itself has a significant spiritual impact but we also need to walk in the replacement truth and blessing until it has become part of our everyday life. The initial period is when they are most tenuous so we encourage clients to use every means possible to build these truths into their lives. A few aids to walking in the new way that God has shown you could include

---

[47] Genesis 2:24.

- a partner or close friend perhaps encouraging, reminding and even correcting where they see the person living the old way;
- declaring the truth and blessings;
- placing them somewhere they will be easily seen and brought to mind, for example, on a mirror used for shaving or make-up;
- supplementing the logic of the left side of the brain with the arts and creativity of the right side of the brain.

Illustrations

FROM MY 2017 JOURNAL

I can illustrate how the Paradigm can work in daily life by giving an example, but first I need to set some context for you. Historical: I mentioned previously that when I was two I had an experience that perhaps was acceptable but would now be described as my having been sexually abused. Modern: I was first writing this book two days before Helen and I would go on holiday to Cornwall. My sleep had been increasingly broken as the holiday approached. I journaled as follows.

I woke this Sunday morning feeling pressured. I wanted to know why so began to express my feelings. "I want to mow the lawn and go to St Andrew's. The lawn 'cos it's too long. St Andrews 'cos I enjoy worshipping with them. What do I do with the old copier and computer stuff? Easiest is to throw it away but that is such a waste. VHF needs mastering. Cross-stitch needs doing and the pattern software mastering. Finances are out of date. Go on holiday on Tuesday. Savings are not in good place so losing money for you, Lord."

Possibly prompted by the Spirit the question came to mind, "Why the urgency?"

I have shown the awareness He gave next on pages 111/112. As I looked with the Lord at what I had expressed I saw the following:

Non-godly belief: *1) "I have to have everything tidy."*

2) "She's dangerous and will get me."

3) "I always cause trouble."

4) "I can never be good enough."

5) "It's hopeless" (and I have learnt that most times beneath 'it's' is 'I'm' so this is really "I'm hopeless" i.e. a False Identity Statement.)

6) "I have to keep on trying."

7) "Keeping Mum happy keeps me safe."

So the reality is that I at 66 years old, am under pressure because of these aspects of my operating system which were formed probably by that 2-year-old experience, which means I am trying to keep everything tidy today at 66 out of a 2-year-old child's fear of being attacked by a woman who died several years ago.

So I 5R'd these and God gave me the replacements shown below.

"I have to have everything tidy."

> *In a fallen world that is impossible; be faithful to Jesus now and trust You for the rest.*

"She's dangerous and will get me."

> *(Recognising she no longer can, but other authority figures may) Jesus will uphold me.*

"I always cause trouble."

> *I am a blessing.*

"I can never be good enough."

> *You value me.*

"It's hopeless", really "I'm hopeless."

> *I am kabod (Hebrew for importance, honour, majesty, glory).*

Some of God's replacements, like this one, take some accepting. Of course, it's consistent with replacement number 4 and with Jesus dying on the cross for me. My reluctance to accept it just shows how far apart God's and my views of me can be!

"I have to keep on trying."

Don't be pushed or pulled, follow Jesus.

"Keeping mum happy keeps me safe."

Jesus keeps me safe.

On this occasion there were no family traits that had not previously been dealt with. Over the years I have met Jesus intimately and received His comfort for the deep emotional content behind these cognitions so on this occasion it was largely a case of becoming aware of some non-godly beliefs that needed updating.

Since then I have focussed on these replacements, i.e. putting these updates to my operating system into effect. One practical step was to look at my task list with Jesus and be faithful to follow what He says. To help me implement that, I arranged with Helen to build into our day a ten-minute slot to consider the jobs and together discern which and how Jesus would have me address. I also asked Helen to encourage me to live out of the replacement truth as the Me God Designed, and not the archaic truth of the Me Life Moulded. What a blessing a godly wife is!

My journal entry at end of that day illustrates Jesus' intimacy with us.

> *As icing on the cake, at church this afternoon one of the younger guys had a picture from God for me of a sailing ship and with me amongst its busy crew but I was to step back and allow the natural flow and then the ship would sail more effectively. This reiterated the morning 'message' not to be driven by urgency. Also, typical of God, He knows my favourite sailing is in Tall Ships so He gives a picture of a Tall Ship. He knows us so well and speaks so personally.*

From hip-pocket clients

In a footnote in chapter 6, I explained that some of the illustrations I use do not come from my own story but are what is known in the profession as from 'hip-pocket clients', real life but non-identifiable experiences. I name them for your ease in reading. So here are two that I hope will help you see how this works and the freedom Jesus brings.

A HUSBAND AND FATHER

As Simon pressed the plunger on his toothpaste, he recalled his irritation at his wife squeezing the toothpaste in the middle. He felt glad they no longer used a metal tube so didn't have those arguments. He could have moved on but, knowing that irritation was a 'stone in his shoe' and meant something was going on inside, he later talked to Jesus about that irritation. The Spirit brought back to mind Simon's terror as a four-year-old when his dad lost his temper because Simon had squeezed the tube wrongly. Simon remembered the vow that 'he'd always do it right' and the Spirit showed him that 'it' extended far beyond tubes of toothpaste, how he had judged others who do 'it' wrong, how he had put his family under a straitjacket of doing 'it' right. Simon asked Jesus to show him where He was when Simon's dad terrorised him. Jesus showed Simon that He was in the bathroom standing between Simon and his dad to protect Simon. Simon expressed his feelings and gave them to Jesus who received them tenderly; they mattered because Simon matters to Jesus. Simon forgave Dad, himself and others. He repented of the non-godly belief and vow and received the replacement 'Jesus loves variety'. He later shared that with his wife and children. Over time they all began to enjoy the new freedom variety gave them to do things differently, especially June, their fourteen-year-old, who had been torn between her love of her dad and his outdated ideas.

A COUPLE

Beth could feel her palms being cut by her nails as she strove to keep quiet, but she felt so afraid and a glance showed her that her kiddies in the back were scared too. But Adrian always drove recklessly and became so angry if she said anything. This was their first day out for ages and she didn't want him in a rage so she kept quiet. In her prayer time later on she realised she couldn't cope with this much longer. If something didn't change, she would have to leave for her and the kids' sake. After quite a while Adrian realised Beth was serious so reluctantly agreed to see us. He was shocked when, in the safety of the ministry room, he heard from Beth how terrified she and the children were of his rages. They each asked for personal ministry to work on their own agenda and then ministry together to work on their marriage relationship.

Beth

As she followed her feelings she became aware of abuse from a parent who flew into rages and also that she could not rely on her other parent for protection. She recognised the family trait from her own mother of hiding and over-submission. She saw false identity statements about her own value and worth and also non-godly beliefs she had about fathers. Jesus gave her replacements as she 5R'd these. Beth met Jesus significantly over one memory of abuse and through that learnt she could take her pains to Him and find His comfort. Beth literally rose up into her being as a valued daughter of God and this enabled her to be far more open with Adrian.

Adrian

He found it difficult to access feelings so initially began with looking at his reckless driving. He discovered non-godly beliefs that real men take risks, that fast driving is manly and skilful, that driving is a competition. His replacement truths to care and protect and that godliness obeys were transformative. He soon realised he needed more skill and character to abide by speed limits than to break them. Looking at his belief that driving was a competition, he became aware of believing he had to beat his older brother who was favoured. As is often the case, beneath Adrian's anger lay great pain. Not only had his father not modelled appropriate emotional literacy, but he being a child of parents who suffered in the world wars when you had to 'grin and bear it', there was a family trait that emotion was unmanly and dangerous, bad for morale. Once Adrian repented on behalf of his family of that trait and received the blessing that emotion brings richness, he was enabled to bring to Jesus the pain of always being second best and receive Jesus' comfort and the truth of his own value. Over time he was able to release archaic pain to Jesus as the Spirit drew it to his attention. This increasingly depowered the non-godly beliefs and he was able to live out the replacements God gave.

Beth and Adrian

In ministry together, they learnt practical outworking of being in a marriage that was a covenant unity rather than a contract, and of communication rather than mere talking. Adrian learnt more of what living with him was really like – very different from how he imagined it to be for his wife and children! Beth realised the depth of pain and insecurity Adrian carried and how her withdrawal had played into those. As Beth became less cowed and withdrawn, and Adrian more emotionally aware, their love was renewed. Jesus revealed His original designs for each of them, their marriage and their children, and they began to live more fruitfully. There were still difficulties but they were better able to surmount them together in the Spirit.

A WARNING FOR MEN

What follows are generalisations but many couples have found them helpful. It's best to read these and see if they resonate with your own experience. Women tend to be more spiritually aware, place a high value on relationship and are emotionally vibrant. Men tend to be more task-orientated, be that their career or their ministry, place a high value on success and favour cognitions of reason, to the extent that some, like I was for my first forty years, are barely emotionally literate.

Single women will enjoy emotionally rich relationships with their girlfriends. Courting, engagement and marriage are also emotionally rich. After a while, however, especially when the couple have children, with the consequent difficulties in finding 'couple time' and the man's impulse to provide, the wife can feel as if she is living in an emotional desert. If she is a godly woman to whom marriage is for life, and divorce anathema, she may cope with this for a long, long time but she will try to get her husband to relate to her emotionally. His emotional illiteracy may mean he does not read her signals. If he continues not to respond, the time can come when she is literally exhausted by living in the desert and for her own sanity feels she has no alternative but to leave him.

We have had several couples where, to be honest, the wife has withstood a degree of relational neglect that amounted to abuse. When she has finally left, or forced him out, the husband has been incredibly surprised. He never realised how hard life had been for her, although with hindsight he sees clearly how he had neglected her and ignored her cries for relationship. Never have we seen a husband who intended to neglect his wife. Each was just living as seemed right to him, on that common land we recognised in chapter 12.

We have seen these husbands work very determinedly to change, to follow the Spirit in updating their operating system, in order to restore their marriage. In one case that worked and the couple reconciled. In another he changed but she was unwilling to examine her own agenda so they separated, fairly amicably but to his intense regret. In other cases, it has been too late. That is the danger for husbands. The godlier your wife, the longer she is likely to endure neglect, some to the extent that they lose all hope and even the husband's transformation is not enough.

Please men, become emotionally literate; love your wives, especially if they are godly.

Please wives, don't simply grin and bear it. Find a way to help your husband to understand. Perhaps get him to read this section, telling him this is where your relationship is heading despite all you are doing. Ask him to work with you to bring water into your desert.

Exercise

1) If you have done the exercise at the end of chapter 8, you will have a list of negative foundational traits. If you have done the exercises in chapter 9, you will have a list of judgements and non-godly beliefs. You could begin to 5R those, receive the Lord's replacements and start to follow Jesus in His new way in those areas of your life.

2) Begin to practise walking in the Spirit with sensitivity to follow the clues He helps you notice in your speech, thought and emotional life. Again, begin to 5R those, receive the Lord's replacements and start to follow Jesus in His new way in those areas of your life.

3) Enlist the aid of a trusted friend or spouse to encourage you to walk in the new ways of truth, then notice and rejoice in the new life that fruits.

Conclusion

You know how you take great care in choosing a particular picture to fit with your decor. You buy it, take it home, mount it and revel in it. Two years later you invite into your home a new friend who admires the picture and, although you don't say anything, you realise that you have not actually seen it for a considerable length of time. It has just become part of your background and has lost the special significance it held for you.

There may be some new insights here for those who are not familiar with psychology, neurology and cognitive development, but the key principles are as old as the scriptures from which they come.

> *And we all, who with unveiled faces contemplate the Lord's glory, are being transformed into his image with ever-increasing glory, which comes from the Lord, who is the Spirit.*
>
> *2 Corinthians 3:18*

> *"...Whoever wants to be my disciple must deny themselves and take up their cross daily and follow me."*
>
> *Luke 9:23*

> *Therefore do not let sin reign in your mortal bodies so that you obey its evil desires.*
>
> *Romans 6:12*

> *The law of the spirit of life has set me free from the law of sin and death.*
>
> *Romans 8:2*

> *As for you, you were dead in your transgressions and sins, in which used to live when you followed the ways of this world and of the ruler of the kingdom of the air, the spirit who is now at work in those who are disobedient. All of us also lived among them at one time, gratifying the cravings of our sinful nature and following its desires and thoughts. Like the rest, we were by nature objects of wrath. But because of his great love for us, God, who is rich in mercy, made us alive with*

Christ even when we were dead in transgressions – it is by grace you have been saved. And God raised up with Christ and seated us with him in the heavenly realms in Christ Jesus ... For we are God's workmanship, created in Christ Jesus to do good works, which God prepared in advance for us to do.

Ephesians 2:1-10

So I say, live by the Spirit, and you will not gratify the desires of the sinful nature. For the sinful nature desires what is contrary to the spirit, and the spirit what is contrary to the sinful nature. They are in conflict with each other, so that you do not do what you want.

Galatians 5:16,17

Sadly, like the picture we hung on our wall, the scriptures can lose their significance so that we reduce their meaning, and also their benefit. My hope is that in expressing these principles in more modern language, familiar scriptures will regain their intended impact.

All Scripture is God-breathed and is useful for teaching, rebuking, correcting and training in righteousness, so that the man of God may be thoroughly equipped for every good work.

2 Timothy 3:16,17

My prayer is that the different language will be used by the Spirit to help each of us walk in the truth of scripture.

I do encourage you that these principles and tools have been prayed through, taught by the Spirit and used by Him to bring radical change into many people's lives. They have:

- found greater intimacy with Jesus;
- experienced renewed marriages, and relationships within family and church;
- had greater awareness of their value, worth and design;
- moved more proactively into their destiny to be channels of Jesus' love to those around them.

May that be your experience also.

Finally, whilst I was writing this book I came across a hymn written by F. Bottome (c. 1870) which expresses our heart cry.

Search me, O God, my actions try,
And let my life appear
As seen by Thine all-searching eye:
To mine my ways make clear.

Search all my sense and know my heart,
Who only canst make known,
And let the deep, the hidden part
To me be fully shown.

Throw light into the darkened cells,
Where passion reigns within;
Quicken my conscience till it feels
The loathsomeness of sin.

Search all my thoughts, the secret springs,
The motives that control,
The chambers where polluted things
Hold Empire o'er the soul.

Search till Thy fiery glance has cast
Its holy light through all,
And I by grace am brought at last
Before Thy face to fall.

Thus prostrate I shall learn of thee
What now I feebly prove,
That God alone in Christ can be
Unutterable love!

Only by Jesus living in us, transforming us, can we be channels of unutterable love to those around us. May this book help you to live intimately with Jesus as the You God Designed, fulfilling the unique destiny He has prepared for you to walk in, to the glory and praise of Jesus our loving and lovely Lord. May His acclamation ring over you, "Well done, good and faithful servant!"

Appendix

We gratefully acknowledge that the following is a distillation of principles and practices we have learnt from many sources including Freedom in Christ, Jesus Ministry, Restoring the Foundations Ministry and *A More Excellent Way* by Henry W. Wright.

Bespoke Ministry Prayer Aide – Holistic [5R] Prayer

This is intended to help you pray into an issue the Lord has brought to your attention. We hope that you would be able to pray the principles in your own words and soon not need this aide. It will have failed if it becomes liturgical or rote or a religious practice. Jesus wants to meet you in a love-tryst, not in a ritual!

The prayer is in italics. In ordinary type are directions and alternatives to be used depending upon what you are praying about.

HISTORICAL AND COGNITIVE (BELIEFS)

Recognise

Thank you, Holy Spirit, for showing me

{Historical: *the sin of _____ in my family line.*}

{Cognition: *the non-godly belief that _____.*}

I know this is not Your way.

Repent

I repent of that and renounce it and

{Historical: *all its effects in my life and line.*}

{Cognition: *the way I have believed, behaved and judged others by it.*}

I declare that I will walk in Your truth.

Well done, good and faithful servant!

Release and receive

I forgive

{Historical: *all those in my family line who lived in this,*}

{Cognition: *all those who in any way played any part in my living by this lie,*}

especially _____ [name anyone God brings to mind].
I forgive myself.
I ask You to forgive me, Lord.
Because of your cross and resurrection I receive Your forgiveness. [Pause to do so.]

Rebuke

In the Name and Authority of Jesus Christ

{Vow/curse/judgement: *I take the sword of the Spirit and break this* [vow/curse/judgement].}

{Unhealthy soul ties: *I take the sword of the Spirit and sever the unhealthy soul tie between me and [name].*}

I command all spirits empowering this [vow/curse/judgement/unhealthy soul tie] *and associated with this sin off my life, to go under the feet of Jesus and not to return.*}

{Unhealthy soul ties: *I release myself to be wholly myself free from* [name], *and* [name] *to be wholly himself/herself free from me.*}

Replace

Thank you for your freedom, Lord. Please fill every area of my life that has been affected by this sin with your Holy Spirit. [Pause to receive Him.]
Please show me your replacement in which you want me to live from now on. [Pause to hear – if a godly belief, make it concise.]

Thank you, Father, for [the replacement] *in which you wish me to walk.*
Please fill every area of my life that the sin affected with [the replacement] *and empower me to live in* [the replacement] *from now on.*
[In this part of the prayer the replacement is mentioned three times as a good start to building the new neurological pattern in your brain.]

EMOTIONAL

Recognise

Dear Holy Spirit,

{For past emotional disturbance: *please help me be in that place again.*}

{For current: emotional disturbance: *please help me see what is going on here.*}

Please help me to become aware of, and pour out to you, all I feel about this.
[Be honest and real with Jesus. He is unshockable and already knows. It is as you honestly express yourself that you will recognise your wound. It may help to write what you feel or, if praying with someone, for them to write what you say.]

Release

Lord Jesus, I give to you all these feelings, my _____ [name each one and when all have been given to Jesus, be aware of His response].

Receive

Lord Jesus, please show me where you were when this happened and please show me your perspective on it.
[Respond to what He shows you.]
[Forgive anyone who needs forgiving and

deal with any Historical and Cognitive aspects of which you became aware.]

Rebuke

In the Name and Authority of Jesus Christ, I command all spirits which have had a place in my life due to this wounding, off my life, to go under the feet of Jesus and not to return.

Return

[Ask the Holy Spirit to take you back to the original place and see how it is. It will usually be wholly transformed but there may still be more work to do. If there is, ask Him if that is for now or later and act accordingly.]

Replace

[Thank Jesus for the healing, presence and perspective He showed you.] *Please fill every area affected by this wounding with* [healing, presence and perspective He showed you] *and please empower me to live in those truths from now on.*

Spiritual

[This is prayed as part of the other aspects as the Lord leads.]

What Shall I Read Next?

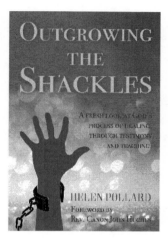

Outgrowing the Shackles

Helen Pollard
ISBN 978-1-78815-669-1

Emotional healing is often a process. God, in His infinite love and wisdom, addresses issues in our hearts in His own timing and not necessarily in the order we might choose. The freedom He brings us is not usually an instantaneous event, but a result of our growth and maturing as we allow Him to gentle touch every area of our lives.

Helen Pollard survived a traumatic childhood through Jesus' miraculous healing, alongside help from secular therapies and varied prayer ministries. In this book she uses her own story to guide us into principles that we can apply to our own lives – to outgrow the shackles. Helen's blunt realism is disarming, whilst her profound wisdom and insight into healing and forgiveness are a challenge to every believer.

Available from your local bookshop.

For more information, visit:
www.onwardsandupwards.org/**outgrowing-the-shackles**